making money on the net made painless

College of Advanced Studies
102-105 Whitechapel High Street
London E1 7RA
Tel: +44(0)207 3779888
Fax: +44(0)207 3779466

The Commonwealth Law College Ltd.
Reg: 4583015
Danai Choudhary, Lawyer (Managing Directors)
Register Office
6 Commercial Street, London, E1 6LP.
Tel: 020 7247 0085 Fax: 020 7247 7331

THIS IS A CARLTON BOOK

Text and design copyright © Carlton Books 2000

This book is sold subject to the condition that it shall not, by way of trade or otherwise, be lent, resold, hired out or otherwise circulated without the publisher's prior written consent in any form of cover or binding other than that in which it is published and without a similar condition, including this condition, being imposed upon the subsequent purchaser. All rights reserved.

A CIP catalogue record for this book is available from the British Library

ISBN 1 84222 224 4

Project Editor: Lara Maiklem
Production: Sarah Corteel

Created by Gecko Grafx Ltd

Notice of liability
Every effort has been made to ensure that this book contains accurate and current information. However, the publisher and the author shall not be liable for any loss or damage suffered by the readers as a result of any information contained herein.

Trademarks
All company trademarks are acknowledged as belonging to their respective companies.

Printed and bound in Italy

making money on the net
made painless

Christophe Dillinger

CARLTON BOOKS

CONTENTS

INTRODUCTION — 6

CHAPTER 01	GREAT IDEAS	8
CHAPTER 02	WAYS TO MAKE MONEY	20
CHAPTER 03	INTERNET BRANDING	32
CHAPTER 04	SETTING UP YOUR E-BUSINESS	38
CHAPTER 05	DESIGNING YOUR WEB SITE	47
CHAPTER 06	WEB STRATEGIES	56
CHAPTER 07	DELIVERING CUSTOMER SERVICE	62
CHAPTER 08	PROMOTING YOUR WEB SITE	71
CHAPTER 09	SELLING ADVERTISING SPACE AND EMAIL ADDRESSES	79
CHAPTER 10	EXPANDING YOUR BUSINESS	88
CHAPTER 11	SELLING YOUR SITE	95

CHAPTER 12	USING A WEB SITE TO ENHANCE YOUR CURRENT BUSINESS	104
CHAPTER 13	GET PAID TO SURF	110
CHAPTER 14	THE DOMAIN NAME GAME	116
CHAPTER 15	YOUR FINANCES MADE EASY – BANKING ON THE NET	128
CHAPTER 16	GETTING A JOB	134
CHAPTER 17	ONLINE AUCTIONS	143
CHAPTER 18	BUYING AND SELLING SHARES	155
CHAPTER 19	ONLINE GAMBLING	164
CHAPTER 20	BUYING AND SELLING YOUR HOME	170
CHAPTER 21	SHOPPING	176

INDEX   188

INTRODUCTION

The Internet is changing the world, right in front of our eyes. It is the greatest encyclopaedia-catalogue-dictionary-news report-entertainment centre-resource that mankind has ever seen. It's also the most exciting new global financial opportunity in history. Everything you could possibly want is available on the Net somewhere, if you can find it – and it has a price. It's impossible to tell accurately how much money is made on the web worldwide in a given year, but conservative estimates suggest that ecommerce was worth $50 billion in the 1999/2000 tax year, and it could be worth ten times as much again in 2000/2001.

More and more, people are turning to the Internet to find levels of convenience, choice and speed that they could never dream of in their local shopping centre. You can do your shopping, go to the races or the casino, sell your house, do the banking, find a new job, search the auctions for bargains and even buy wholesale, all without leaving your living room. The savings that you can make are potentially incredible.

Businesses are using the Internet to source all their requirements, from printed stationery and furniture to experts and new employees. If your company does not have a well-designed, informative web-site that explains who you are and what you do, you're cutting yourself off from as much as 40 per cent of your target business. Similarly, people with product to sell are finding that they can reach up to a tenth of the world's population on the Internet, and more every day – something totally undreamed of by advertising agencies even five years ago.

But it's not just existing businesses that can make money on the web. In fact, some of the greatest financial rewards have gone to people looking to start up a new idea from scratch. It has been the stockmarket flotation of some of these so-called 'dotcom startups' that has really captured the media's attention. When bright teenagers and twenty-somethings with a bit of savvy can find themselves on the receiving end of millions of pounds to start an ebusiness empire – and hundreds, even thousands of them already have – then everyone can see that there is money to be made. A few of the companies have gone spectacularly bust, but a lot more continue to make fortunes for their founders.

It's not all just a matter of sticking up a web page, though. You have to have a clear idea of the way that you intend to make money from the Internet, and make sure that you design a web-site that fits with that idea. You need to have an idea about the people you want to come to your site, and find ways to tempt them in to you – because there are an awful lot of other sites out there, too. You'll need to make sure that your site is totally user-friendly, because the watchword of the web is convenience, and you may have as little as three or four seconds to grab a surfer's or a potential client's attention. However, with a little bit of thought, a solid idea, a good name and an aggressive marketing strategy, you'll be well placed to start reaping some of the rewards that the Internet has to offer.

Perhaps more vitally, the fact is that the Internet is here to stay, and its importance is just going to keep growing. There's nothing we can do to change that now. It's a global marketplace and it is going to revolutionize the business world. When the change comes, you need to be placed to take advantage of it, not to be swept away by it, and that means getting familiar with business on the web as soon as you can. This book will show you how to do just that.

Welcome to the most exciting ride of our lives.

GREAT IDEAS

We'll start off our survey of electronic commerce by looking at some of the most successful and/or innovative sites to be found around the world on the web. Some you will no doubt know, while others may be more of a surprise.

AMAZON BOOKSTORE REVIEW SITE

URL: http://www.amazon.com
or: http://www.amazon.co.uk

Amazon is, arguably, the best-known retail web-site on the Net. It was one of the first internet retailers to be heavily publicized. Although they began as an online bookstore, Amazon have since diversified into a multitude of media, products, goods and services. From Amazon you can now buy anything from cosmetics to chainsaws.

Books were an excellent start up product for a number of reasons: they are non-perishable, requiring only inexpensive warehousing. People are already accustomed to ordering books – especially in the light of the shrinking lists of many high street and provincial bookstores. Importantly, the market niche was largely under-exploited.

The real advantage that Amazon offers over conventional shops and catalogues is the possibility of reading reviews for every product. Reviews come in two forms: editorial reviews, from Amazon staff, and customer reviews, from people who have already bought and tried the goods. Other useful features on offer include 'Purchase Circles'. These are highly specialized best-seller lists specific to criteria such as your profession, hobby or even post-code.

Obviously the main turnover for Amazon is generated by retail sales. The challenge is to persuade people to buy online rather than using more conventional methods. To this end, the purchasing process must be as straightforward as possible and the delivery schedule prompt to retain repeat custom. Another means toward the end of customer retention is the option to have Amazon keep your details and records of your purchases in order to generate a (private) profile of your interests. Subsequently, the software may be able to suggest items which are most likely to be of interest to you.

IMDB DATABASE INFO SITE

URL: http://www.imbd.com

The Internet Movie Database (IMDb) is part of the same group of companies as Amazon.com. It is a sponsored site, supported by advertising. To attract advertising revenue, a site must supply to the public or an industry information which is in wide demand, and ideally be able to target adverts at a known user-profile, ie the age and earnings category most likely to buy their product.

IMDb: a great reference site

In the case of the IMDB, the product is movie information. In minute detail. The site is extremely popular with both the general film-going public and all sorts of workers in the film industry. The database contains the names, cast lists, reviews and hundreds of other details of thousands of films. Did you know that actress Linda Hamilton has a twin sister who appears fleetingly in Terminator II? Now you do. In common with Amazon, the strength of this very successful site lies in reviews. A film-lover could plan a lifetime's worth of viewing from their browser, cross-referencing their favourite genres, directors, actors or even stunt-doubles using IMDB's powerful search engine.

Not all content is generated in-house. IMDB boasts 30,000 links to external sites which provide reviews, clips and other goodies. There are also links to sponsors' sites and to co-operating organizations which supply related content, goods and services. DVDs, VHS video, soundtracks and books can be ordered direct from the IMDb site itself or via links to the vendors' sites.

The popularity of this site, as well as the tight focus of its user profile (they watch or make movies of a known type), makes the IMDb site a hot property.

FREESERVE PORTAL

URL: http://www.freeserve.com

Freeserve was one of the first UK ISPs

GREAT IDEAS

(Internet Service Provider) offering connection without a subscription charge. Instead, Freeserve takes a cut of the local call fee paid by the user to their telecoms provider (usually BT). This low-cost feature is, in itself, the biggest customer draw. It allowed Freeserve to build a large client-base very quickly and thereby, hopefully, to attract advertisers.

For advertisers themselves, the Portal page is the most important. While any Internet user can access the Freeserve Portal page, it is always the first page that all Freeserve customers see whenever they log on unless they actively seek to avoid it.

While it is always vital to generate a high hit-rate to any page that is to become valuable as advertising 'virtual-estate', making a page the first thing that the entire customer-base of a popular ISP sees makes it extremely desirable.

Only a relatively small amount of space on the Portal page is given over to external adverts as Freeserve offer a great deal of their own content. Links to feature articles, competitions and their own news pages predominate over the banner ads for sports, holidays and recruitment. Of course the in-house content pages also carry sponsors' banners but not too thickly. This restrained approach not only provides an uncluttered surf for the user but maintains the high value of the advertising space sold.

BABYLON X ADULT SITE

URL: http://www.babylonx.com

Babylon X is an 'adult' site specializing in supplying pictures and video clips of nude celebrities. These range from the type of long-lens paparazzi shots that the tabloids would blush to publish to stolen home-movie footage à la Pamela and Tommy. Standard porn-site fare is also available.

The site is financed by subscription: $29.50 per month after a two-week introductory offer at $2.95. Unlike many other sites of the type, it does not appear to use a third-party AVS (Adult Verification Service) but has its own credit card form. Other payment methods are also accepted, naturally.

Babylon X has a rather aggressive marketing strategy. The pages are themed in the classic bordello livery of black and red. There are a number of links to 'free samples' (thumbnail images) of the currently headlining celebrities. These links funnel the curious inexorably toward the credit card membership form page. Interestingly, the 'back' button of your browser is 'trapped', taking you to a special offer page rather than your previous location. This is a common ploy from Internet pornography sites and they will often dump you onto another, similar site rather than let you go back to where you came from, the idea being that a change is as good as a rest, and that you'd rather see another porn site than escape from it all.

Given that there are literally hundreds of thousands of porn sites on the Net, sadly their money-making potential simply cannot be ignored. Many of their ploys for keeping the surfer 'hooked' will no doubt be used by other types of site in the future as the race to get and hold on to prospective customers hots up. Most of these are small, very clever and highly effective Java scripts.

Part of the perceived necessity for this proactive marketing is that it is not as easy to make money from pornography on the Internet as is often suggested. Any original content which is in any kind of demand will immediately be reposted for free elsewhere and most likely harvested to be rebadged by unscrupulous competitors. Lacking exclusivity or some other draw, paid subscriptions will soon be cancelled. Consequently, many sites will also sell VHS videos, DVDs and CD-ROMs of images too large to be conveniently pirated on a low-bandwidth connection.

REUTERS STOCK TICKER UTILITY SITE

URL: http://www.reuters.com

Reuters.com is the web site of the renowned international news agency. From the front page users can choose to view selected articles of news from the categories of: world news, business, web, technology, science, sports, entertainment, human interest and extra sections on events such as the Olympic Games. The site specializes in breaking news and has a global Stock Lookup database that can be used to find the current value of stocks on any exchange. The front page boasts clear graphs of NASDAQ data over the financial year.

The Reuters.com site has no visible means of support, all pages being free to view and carrying no banner adverts. Obviously the available selection of news stories are but a fraction of all the material gathered by this renowned agency. The site, therefore, seems to be Reuters' corporate presence on the web – a public-facing PR page for the media company. Publishers of newspapers could use the site as a point of first contact when approaching Reuters to buy in news stories from them, so it does operate as a business to business advertisement for Reuters in itself, but they have a separate corporate page for this purpose. The site is presented very much as a news service free to all users.

What links there are on the page are to affiliated organizations' sites.

SCOTT ADAMS PROMOTIONAL SITE – DILBERT.COM

URL: http://www.dilbert.com

This is the homepage of Scott Adams' hugely popular comic creation Dilbert, the harassed office worker. Adams' humour satirizes stereotypical office life. Characters in the daily updated strip include Dilbert, a much put-upon employee, Catbert the evil Human Resources manager and Dogbert, the megalomaniacal mutt.

The site offers various Dilbert-related diversions including a cartoon strip archive, a merchandising store, a reader poll, 'inside scoops', a potted bio of the author and various other entertaining features such as a random mission-statement generator. The content is refreshed frequently and fans may subscribe to an e-newsletter.

The immense popularity of the Dilbert cartoon and the potential for repeated and regular custom makes the Dilbert page perfect for advertising. In keeping with the theme of job-dissatisfaction, one of the main sponsors is a recruitment agency. This is an excellent example of a traditionally paper-based product moving successfully into the new media. Furthermore, Dilbert's target audience of office wage-slaves and young professionals has a known user profile and is likely to have web access at work if not at home, improving its value to advertisers. Some of the advertising is quite sophisticated: entering some pages opens a streamed video advertisement, which could be annoying on slow connections.

Another function of the site is as a contact point for those wishing to reprint Dilbert strips or graphics under licence from the copyright holders.

DAVE'S VIDEO GAME CLASSICS TRIBUTE SITE

URL: http://www.davesvgc.com/

Dave's is classic in a number of ways. It is a fansite for classic video games and it is a classic example of a tribute site. Also, in an altogether classic manner, it is currently suspended whilst being sued by a video game manufacturer for copyright infringement.

To work well, a tribute site must concern a topic which has a lreasonably large fan-base of people with some modest spending-power. This appeared for Dave's site when more affluent thirty-somethings began to reminisce about the consoles and video games of their teen years. Remember Vectrex? Remember Colecovision? Many do and yet they still want to play them. Retro-gaming has a small but keen following. Many say that, in the absence of 3Dfx and 128-bit sound, gameplay was everything. Add nostalgia and you're away.

Of course, it is hard to buy functional hardware now, though many people are restoring old arcade consoles. Fortunately, modern computers can easily run emulators of all the old beep-machines – and some not-so-old ones too. Dave's started out as a fan-page where Dave could rhapsodize about the joys of 8-bit graphics and piezo-electric sound-effects, but the site rapidly became a forum for enthusiasts. Once popular enough, it was possible to host adverts for related sites and fanzines.

Problems arose for Dave and his parent company when people started to get 'nostalgic' for consoles or games that are still on the market. When the BIOS of Sony's Playstation was posted on the site, the lawyers pounced. This is a problem that many tribute sites run into. Usually the problem is reproducing a trade-marked graphic or logo without permission, so great care must be taken not to offend the objects of one's enthusiasm.

BATTLE.NET ONLINE GAMING

URL: *http://www.battle.net*

The Battle.net site is not an end in itself, its function being to facilitate the use of the leisure software it supports, namely the games Diablo II, Warcraft and Starcraft from Blizzard Entertainment. There is no subscription charge for use of the site, its upkeep and overheads being built into the initial cost of ownership of the games. Sign-up procedures are initiated from within the game package. For existing players of the games, the site offers a place to meet, chat with and challenge opponents. There are also hints and strategy tips available along with updates and patches to download. For those who do not yet own the games, the site offers reviews, previews and product announcements and an online store selling Blizzard products.

The Battle.net site is mirrored on a number of hosting servers around the world to keep ping times low and allow smooth play (the ping time is the time it takes you to communicate with a remote computer).

Since it carries no external advertising, nor charges for use, the site is not intended to stand alone in a profit-making capacity. Instead it is a part of a much bigger product – multi-player gaming. In the short history of computer games, the single-player game was superseded at the leading edge of the market, first by two-player games then by multi-player LAN or Web-based games. Battle.net offers players a functionally limitless number of potential opponents of various nationalities and skill levels. This potential offers gamers a next generation muti-player experience but it must absolutely be good, because only sustained sales of the game titles will keep the site profitable. A site supporting a limited client-base will swiftly flounder into the red.

LASTMINUTE.COM SALES

URL: http://www.lastminute.com

The lastminute.com site was ingeniously designed to exploit a tricky market niche. Companies such as airlines, travel agents, theatre ticket agencies etc. all deal in commodities with a time-limited value. As the deadline beyond which the product becomes valueless gets nearer, the pressure builds up for the vendor to dispose of it, even at a loss, to offset liabilities. The problem here is that vendors can be extremely reluctant to be seen to be discounting heavily outside of planned promotions. This reflects badly on vendors as customers may assume that the company is badly run or in crisis. Also regular clearance discounting may influence customer behaviour, encouraging them to hangfire on purchasing, knowing they can buy at knockdown prices later. The solution offered by middle-man brokers like lastminute.com insulates the vendor from embarrassment. As a result, lastminute witholds the identity of the vendor and, indeed, the size of the discount from the buyer until after payment has been made. Also, this enables lastminute to pitch their advertising at people looking for short-notice 'spontaneous' travel while not forgetting those shopping in an emergency or simply budgeting.

While it seems like a perfect scheme, the margins are bound to be quite low and the advertising requirements quite high. Lastminute needs to become a household name and encourage 'spontaneous, romantic and sometimes adventurous behaviour' in their prospective clients, and overcome the public's natural suspicion of parting with large sums over the Internet. Conversely, the staff and premises overheads can be kept low.

THE ONION MAGAZINE SITE

URL: http://www.theonion.com

Billing itself as 'America's finest news source', the Onion site is an online version of a satirical spoof newspaper which lampoons the style and content of middle-American media. The humour tends towards the ironic, which is refreshing in a US site.

The film reviews are not tongue-in-cheek and are quite good but the hilarious problem page with its sour and grumpy agony uncle is somewhat lewd and not for the shockable. From the site, readers can also buy Onion merchandise or subscribe to the paper version which is 30 per cent greater in terms of content.

The Onion leans heavily towards music, film and entertainments media, these comprising its only serious content in the form of The Onion Audio-Visual Club. The rest is pure silliness of varied depth and intelligence, not entirely unakin to a grown-up *Mad* magazine or the middle pages of *Private Eye*.

The Onion site works the same way as any free paper or magazine but without the printing overheads. Customers are attracted repeatedly to the site by frequently refreshed, entertaining content which makes the pages valuable advertising real-estate. The advantage to the advertiser over paper-based versions of a publication is that within a few mouse-clicks prospective customers can be purchasing your product rather than needing to telephone or post orders via snail-mail.

FRAMSTICKS

URL: http://www.frams.poznan.pl/

One of Maciej Kominski's creatures...

Framsticks is the web page of Maciej Kominski, a post-graduate research student at Poznan University in Poland.

His research project is an artificial life (ALife) simulator named Framsticks.

The program is downloadable as shareware, allowing users to design their own surprisingly complex virtual creatures from rod-shaped components to which may be added sensors, neurones or actuators (muscles). The creatures, called 'Frams', may then be let loose in a user-defined, physics-modelled environment to multiply, compete and evolve. The animation in the shareware version is simple but, for a price, a registration code sent by email will unlock an OpenGL animation feature which is much more pleasing. Also, the program can output frame-by-frame scene files which can be rendered in a popular ray-tracing engine to produce startling animation, many of which have been uploaded to the site by proud users for all to see.

It is unlikely that Maciej will do more than offset his expenses with the income from this site. He uses a third-party ecommerce provider to process his orders. The site is more a labour of love than an economic proposition, but it is well designed and attractive with a pleasant music track as background. All the documentation and tech-specs of the program are on the site, along with more background on ALife. The page also acts as a forum for Framsticks fans.

SHAREWARE.COM

URL: http://shareware.cnet.com

Shareware.com is part of the huge CNET online technology market. The site holds a massive collection of freeware, shareware and demo licensed programs for all platforms and OSs including Amiga. Dozens more are added daily. There are more categories than can be usefully mentioned here, but they include everything you might expect, from mainstream game demos and beta version to patches, desktop themes and multimedia tools.

The list is fully searchable, enabling you to cross-reference platform, operating system, licence and any keywords. Files are accompanied by brief descriptions of program and publisher with user reviews where available. These reviews record the number of times an item has been downloaded and a simple percentage of 'thumbs-up' and 'thumbs-down' from responding users. The site offers a variety of specialized e-newsletters to advise subscribers of new products. All CNET sites are garnished with unobtrusive banner-type ads and shareware.com presumably takes a percentage of any registration fees paid to publishers as a result of downloads from their pages.

The ease of use and plethora of available titles makes the site an excellent resource no matter what your field of interest. It is a great place to get things in a hurry. Need a program to stitch Targa image files into an .AVI or .MPG? Need to view a bizarre file format? Today? A site like shareware.com is a good first port of call.

OPEN.GOV.UK

URL: http://www.open.gov.uk

Notwithstanding the accusations of obsessive secrecy and chicanery often levelled at Tony Blair's British government, open.gov.uk is the name of the official UK Government services website. It advertises itself as 'the first point of contact to UK Public Services info on the Web'.

From the front page, users can search the 'Pathfinder' list of other UK Government portals. There are alphabetical links leading to lists of respective categories and a topic index. The 'What's New' page lists recent changes to legislation and service provision.

The colour scheme of the site is grey, possibly in reference to the stoney shades of municipal architecture, and blue which is a colour suggestive of security and reliability – much used in banking commercials. It is maintained by Central Computer & Telecommunications Agency.

Accusations could be made that not enough effort has been put into adapting the delivery of information to a web-based format. Many documents are in Adobe Acrobat format (requiring a viewer to be downloaded if not already installed) rather than in HTML which seems like an obvious choice. Another issue is that, although the indexes on the front page make finding documents in any given category easy, there are few links from within documents to related topics under other categories.

It would, of course, be unseemly for a government site to advertise anything but their own services. It's not impossible that we might, one day, see a banner advert for Andersen Consulting or BP adorning the pages of .gov sites. Until then, it remains a state-funded public service.

AKUPUNK.COM

URL: http://www.akupunk.com

Akupunk.com is, as you might guess, concerned with acupuncture. It is the web site of Andrew Gordon, a practitioner of traditional chinese medicine. Clearly, the prime function of the site is to advertise Mr Gordon's practice to the web-searching public. An increasing number of people are turning to web search-engines as opposed to the Yellow Pages when looking for such services. A web page can contain far more information than any printed advertisement.

Efforts have been made to make the pages a useful resource for clients, practitioners and students of TCM. There is a feedback form and an announcements board for existing clients. Prospective clients can learn more about the principles of TCM from the clear and detailed explanatory pages before making an appointment through a form or by email.

Practitioners and students can sign the guestbook or research patent remedies in the 'lotions, potions and pills' section. There is also news covering up-to-date legislation affecting the industry. Akupunk.com carries no advertising, beyond mentioning that Mr Gordon is a rep for a large herbal-medicine importer. The potential to attract advertisers is there, however, if the page can attract enough practitioners.

Sole-trader web sites like this can range from being little more than a business card to rivalling the content of major players. In their smallest form, they serve only to announce the trader's presence on the Net and to web directories and search engines thereby, hopefully, gaining profitable clients. If, however, they offer content attractive to both their customers and peers – especially if that content is updated regularly to get repeat visits – then the potential arises to get other companies or traders to pay for advertising space on the site. This way, the site will reimburse the labour required for its maintenance, or even become directly profitable.

SINCLAIR RESEARCH

URL: http://www.sinclair-research.co.uk

Everyone over 30 will remember Sir Clive Sinclair. Without him, you might be a great deal more surprised to see a computer in your house. It would still be there – you would just be more surprised than you probably are. Though the bloodline of Sinclair's home computers withered at roughly the same time that Intel were turning out the 80286 processor, it was Sir Clive who made the concept of an affordable home computer seem real. He is, perhaps, more notorious than famous for his abortive attempt to break into the electric vehicle market with his ill-fated tricycle travel pod, the C5.

In the technological wilderness for

years, knocking out CD-ROMs mail order from his front room, the irrepressible egghead is back. Through his shiny new web site, he is selling his latest electronic innovations: two tiny radios and an electric motor for bicycles. Sinclair's trademark obsession with miniaturization is well evident here as both the AM and FM radios, described as the world's smallest, are no bigger than a man's thumb-tip and fit directly into the ear.

Transactions take place through Shop@ssistant software courtesy of Vector Services who maintain the site. Making purchases is swift and pretty straightforward.

Though neatly designed and attractive, the site, oddly, offers no real customer service, delegating such things to Vector. There is only a snail-mail address for enquiries direct to Sinclair Research. It seems that Sir Clive is missing out on the opportunity to capitalize on his (once high) public profile to increase possible brand awareness.

CNET

URL: http://www.cnet.com

CNET is an award-winning new media company – the 15th largest on the Net – with its fingers in the pies of TV and radio. CNET specializes in science and technology news and the tech-related aspects of business and recruitment.

In terms of shopping (mainly computer and electronics), the CNET page boasts a search engine, a directory of online auctions, product reviews and comparison shopping. Comparison shopping looks like the future of online buying. On the CNET shopping pages, users may browse the prices for any given article quoted by dozens of participating vendors and add items to their CNET virtual shopping-basket with the click of a mouse. Although only one order and payment are made, the individual orders to multiple vendors are forwarded by CNET to be delivered by the vendor(s). Prices are checked and updated twice daily.

CNET is a big business with big financing. Advertising is not overdone, being confined to a banner ad and one or two links per page. The big draw for customers is the up-to-date news, reviews, offers and opportunities reachable via the page. Sadly, CNET does not yet have a UK-based page, so the comparison shopping feature is not useful to UK users, but the information content and downloadable files (see shareware.com, above) make it worth looking at.

WAYS TO MAKE MONEY

E-commerce is an extremely varied field. As the previous chapter shows, successful sites come in a broad range of different styles, and make money from visitors in different ways. They all have the same basic set of goals in common though – the key to running a successful e-business is to get people to come to your site, to stay there long enough to discover what you have on offer, and then to do whatever it is that you need them to do in order to make some cash. That can vary widely, from just staying long enough for their hit to register on your page, to checking through your online catalogue and making a credit card purchase.

One of the first things that you have to do when setting up an ebusiness is to decide how you plan to make money from your site, and then gear everything to making sure that your chosen revenue generation method is made as easy and attractive to visitors as possible. If you don't have a clear idea of how your site is supposed to make money, then the chances are that it never will, regardless of how innovative, attractive or entertaining it is. While many of the traditional ways that companies have of making money translate well to the Internet – product sale, for example – there are others, such as selling information, that are a lot more complicated than you might expect.

Because of this, you need to put some thought into exactly what it is that makes your site a commercially viable proposition. While the web is a huge growth market for businesses at the moment, it is still a commercial marketplace and you need to apply the same sort of rigorous business practices to starting an ecommerce site as you would to starting any other small business. Otherwise, you'll find that the hard work and money that you have put into your site are wasted. There's more to e-commerce than just putting a webpage up and hoping people will start paying you money. There's no need to worry, though. As long as you consider each step of the process, as laid out in this section of the book, you'll be set up to do well.

Just as there are a number of different ways of making money from a web site, so there are a range of different types of site, each tuned to make the most of a particular form of generating cash. As a first priority, you should read through them and decide which type of site you are going to run.

TRIBUTE SITES

A tribute site is the simplest web site of all and was one of the first types of site to appear. Even now, there are more of this type of site than any other, because they are simple and easy to put up. A tribute site is simply a collection of information and links about a specific subject. This category includes home pages, fan sites and any other site where the owner really just wants to share his or her knowledge and/or passion with the world. Subjects on offer can be as specific as a certain character from a book or film, as personal as 'My Family', or as general as jokes and tricks.

Design and illustration is usually pretty basic, because the creator is concerned mainly with getting their information across rather than producing a clever site or making allowance for web analysis and promotion tools. Anything that gets in the way of the core subject is usually left out altogether; a true tribute site has no advertising banners or subscription areas. Links pages to other sites containing information on the same subject are almost a standard requirement and, although these are mostly text links, they may include some banner-style links too. Updates are often infrequent or non-existent, so many of these sites are months or even years old.

The good news is that producing a tribute site is easy. Just assemble as much information as you can about the subject you want to discuss, collect it into themed pages, put in an introduction and an index page, and then publish it. The bad news is that it has almost no potential to generate money. The only way a tribute site can generate cash is to be purchased by a larger company. Attempting to add revenue-generating streams to this sort of site greatly alienates the target audience, who feel – usually quite rightly – that they can find the information elsewhere for free. Although they are modest and unambitious, tribute sites should be treated with respect, because they are a labour of love, and they are the ones that actually make up the huge pool of information that is the backbone of the web. No matter what your interest, enthusiasm or hobby, someone will have produced a tribute site about it somewhere.

For an example of a tribute site, visit http://www.topcities.com/OuterSpace/farshores/farshores/

PROMOTIONAL SITES

A promotional site is similar in basic appearance to a tribute site, but it serves an entirely different purpose. Where a tribute site seeks only to share information that interests the creator, a promotional site is designed to show off the creator's talents, wares, company or skills. It is in the nature of an online portfolio, gallery, showcase or demonstration. Typically, promotional sites either promote something actual, such as a product or company, or hold samples that demonstrate an ability or professional skill, whether it is writing, web design or musical composition.

Promotional sites need to be as attractively designed as possible, so that they look professional, and they need to include full contact details so that if a surfer or a visitor is impressed by what they see, they know where to go. Obviously, including as much information and material as can be usefully provided about the subject is extremely important, and it should be well organized with clear site maps and easily legible web pages, so that potential clients do not run out of patience. If the site is promoting a company, it is important to include an overview of what the company does, full details of the product range, business terms, corporate information, location and so on.

Aside from that, promotional sites have to follow the same sorts of guidelines about overt attempts to make money as tribute sites – there shouldn't be any. A promotional site is designed exclusively to draw attention to yourself or your company, and advertising banners, membership forms, requests for visitor email addresses and other web marketing tools will generate a lot of bad feeling towards you. The creator of a promotional site needs to think of visitors as doing them a favour, rather than vice versa, and so make sure that the favour is repaid as well as possible by not being invasive.

One thing you can do that works well is to add value to the promotional side of your site by including relevant tribute information. A fantasy novelist might include a historical discussion of fantasy books, for example, or a list of new releases from major authors, while a post-production bureau might have cast lists, reviews and short, downloadable clips of films that they have worked on – anything, in other words, that would keep people who might be interested in what the creator is promoting on the site for a closer look.

Promotional sites make money by acting as advertising and marketing for the creator's core business that they are promoting. They will not generate any revenue in aid of themselves. Despite this,

A promotional web site needs to look professional, attractive and friendly.

as more and more companies turn to the web for all their sourcing requirements – from widgets to freelancers – promotional sites are becoming increasingly important. The vast majority of real-world company (ie not e-business) web sites that do not actively seek to sell to Web visitors are promotional sites, and – like fax machines in the early 1990s – every business should now have one.

For an example of a promotional site visit http://www.geckografx.com

BANNER SITES

A banner site is the most basic form of true e-business. It provides tightly themed information on pages that also include one or more advertising banners for product or service sites related to the information. Typically, the creator is paid a small amount of money for each visitor that clicks on the banner and goes on to the advertiser's site (called a click-thru), or a larger amount of money for each product or subscription that the advertiser sells to a visitor who reached their site via the original banner (called a sale). Sophisticated programs on the advertiser's site work out which visitor came from which specific banner site, so that the banner site only needs to host the banner in a page without any fancy programming code.

The advertising banners themselves are generally lurid adverts, come in a standard size and format and are extremely easy to add to a web page. The banner site creator will need to enrol onto the advertiser's promotional scheme, which will involve completing a registration process. No advertisers will pay in advance for banner placement on a banner site, and in fact a small minority of unscrupulous advertisers have been known to actually withhold even earnings they've promised. With most companies, a click-thru may earn a cent ($0.01) or even less, while a sale typically earns around a dollar ($1). While the number of banners you can include on any one web page is in theory unlimited, in practice each one takes a certain amount of time to load up on a visitor's browser and contributes to the visitor's irritation. A good rule of thumb is to include no more than five banners on any one page.

It's important to note that banner sites are considerably less surfer-friendly than tribute sites, so banner sites have to offer either material that is highly desirable, or material that cannot be readily obtained on tribute sites or promotional sites. The most successful venues for banner sites are in the grey areas of the web –

pornographic images (particularly 'TGP' thumbnail galleries), videos and sound files, semi-legal software downloads ('warez'), mp3 music downloads, and hacker-related material. It is also possible to run a banner site profitably with up-to-the minute information on a field that is regularly changing, such as sports news, with banner advertising from relevant sales stores. Regardless of the subject matter, banner sites rely on frequent returns from visitors so, to be profitable, they must offer new content on a daily or two-daily basis. With a popular-content site that features 15 or 20 pages updated daily – about 3 hours' work – and is mentioned on a number of listings sites, it is possible to get a million hits a week or more, which will return about $800 a month.

For an example of a banner site, visit http://www.blackwarez.org

SPAM SITES

A spam site is a relative of the banner site, but with one critical – and surprising – difference: it has no useful content at all, just page after page of confusing, misleading links to advertisers and their banners ('spam' is the internet's adopted term for junk mail and other types of intrusive, unwanted advertising). Obviously, such sites get almost no return visitors, relying instead on the fact that just about every visitor to the site will mistakenly yield at least one click-thru.

As well as normal in-page banners, sites like this will typically have pop-up windows that open new pages in your browser, maybe even a lot of them, and more pop-ups will be opened when you try to leave the site. Although they don't generally produce much in the way of income, a lot of people set up spam sites in areas where banner sites get a lot of hits because they don't take any upkeep at all; you can just produce the site and then leave it in place for unwary surfers to fall into, like flies into a spider web. Most spam sites have titles like 'Free Sex Best Ever Pictures', or 'All Top Software Free Here Today'.

If you are considering a spam site, you should be aware that they generate a lot of bad feeling from surfers and you can expect to get angry, critical email (known as 'flames') about the fact. You may also come under attack from hackers, many of whom are in favour of uncluttered surfing. It would not be in anyone's interest to provide you with an example of a spam site.

RESOURCE SITES

Resource sites are the next level of e-business up from banner sites. They come in a number of different types and styles and are devoted to providing some sort of resource to visitors, hence the name. They too make the majority of their money from banner advertising but, unlike the smaller sites, many have agreements by which they are paid a small amount for each time the banner is downloaded to a visitor's computer (known as a 'hit'), rather than by having the visitor click-thru. Some also sell related products, or offer more extensive resources of the type concerned within a members-only area that requires a paid subscription, usually a monthly membership. They tend to be considerably more professional in web design than banner sites. In addition, some sites sell related merchandise, software or memberships. It is of course possible to have a successful web site that offers more than one type of resource, as long as it is designed carefully. Resource sites may provide loads of information, downloads, links, utility functions or entertainment material, and each will be discussed in turn.

INFORMATION RESOURCE SITES

Information resource sites provide current information on a topic that changes fairly rapidly, such as sporting results, stock market information, TV listings, weather patterns, available jobs and so on. They require regular updates according to the nature of the subject they provide information on; a stock market site has to be updated up to every few seconds, while a job site might only need weekly updates. Obviously, constant updates are more expensive to prepare, maintain and administer than regular ones, so sites with a very high topicality (ie, that change constantly, like stock market sites) tend to provide only limited information for free and require membership subscriptions for full access.

Similarly, sites that provide information which is expensive to obtain – company financial analysis, for example – also require paid subscription. Actually running paid memberships is easy as it's all done by the software for you, but we'll cover that later. For an example of an information resource site, visit http://www.nasdaq.com.

DOWNLOAD RESOURCE SITES

Download resource sites tend to be less corporate than information sites, covering things like shareware and freeware (software that you can download to try out for free, or that is even provided free full stop), illegal pirate 'warez' software, MP3 music files (computer recordings of CD tracks) and other sound clips, picture images (pornographic or otherwise) and video images (ditto).

Because the subject matter is usually of mass appeal to the Internet population, many of these sites do very well, particularly the ones that use generous free samples to sell subscriptions. However, they have to compete with the free material that can be obtained from banner sites. That means that download sites need to have either unique, high-quality content that cannot be found elsewhere – specifically researched information, extensive, easily searched archives, commissioned reports or photosets, actual live content (referred to as 'streaming video'), regular updates, reviews or other such value-added elements. For an example of a download resource site, visit http://www.driverguide.com.

LINKS RESOURCE SITES

Most links resource sites are extremely simple and are half-way towards being banner sites. They tend to just hold links to other sites on the web, generally on a specific theme. The links are usually grouped into categories to make things easier and may include full search functions and/or small reviews for each site. They have to be kept up to date, which means that each link in the database should be manually checked either once or twice a week, and non-functioning ('dead') links removed. Sometimes, the links listed on the site can double as click-thru or sales banners, increasing the site's cashflow. For an example of a links resource site, visit http://www.swiss-magic.ch/resource.html

UTILITY RESOURCE SITES

Utility resource sites provide web-based services that are not easily accessible on other sites, or that may require a large amount of work to set up. Successful examples include a fully searchable on-line King James Bible, a best train route calculator, online dictionaries and encyclopedias, a database of world myths and legends, wine reviews, news clipping services, local area resource guides and much, much more. Some of these sites require a paid subscription, but many others do not, relying on banner advertising, or even offering the material as a charitable or promotional service.

Although some utility resource sites come close in content to information sites (although the material contained, once added, tends to stay valid), others are quite radically different. Utility sites are a diverse bunch, but contain some of the most interesting material to be found on the web. For an example of a utility resource site, visit http://www.thelivinggod.com/kjvbible.htm

ENTERTAINMENT RESOURCE SITES

Entertainment resource sites have a similar broad range of styles and contents as utility sites, varying from the fairly informative through to the downright unusual, but they are dedicated to fun. Some provide entertainment utilities, such as anagram checkers, random Shakespearean insult generators, humorous tests and quizzes and so on, while others have web-based Java games that you can play on your browser. The most ambitious sites provide multi-user games that hundreds or thousands of people can take part in simultaneously, ranging from text-only shared worlds (known as MUDs, short for Multi-User Dimensions) that you can

Get thousands of jokes, delivered to you every single day of the week via email.

participate in with a web browser through to sites supporting the online component of commercial computer games such as Quake and Diablo.

The larger computer game official support sites are often extremely successful, but obviously require a best-selling computer game to drive them on, while MUDs, where people interact virtually in a make-believe setting, are generally run as tribute sites. However, there is plenty of scope for using Java games and other less ambitious entertainment utilities as the backbone of an entertainment site. For an example of an entertainment resource site, visit http://www.funtrivia.com

MAGAZINE RESOURCE SITES

Finally in the resource section, magazine resource sites provide topical information, chat, humorous articles, light entertainment and editorial material, much like a real-world magazine would. They are themed, naturally, concentrating on a specific area of interest. The most successful ones are updated every day with completely new content, keeping archives of old articles. Obviously this requires a lot of work, and large numbers of staff are involved.

Smaller sites may take limited daily updates, or be updated only weekly. These sites tend to make their money from banner advertising, real-world company sponsorship, the sale of their editorial content to syndicated sources, tie-in merchandising like mugs and T-shirts, and other secondary sources. Very few try to get the reader to pay a subscription, because their content is non-critical. Some do include an information resource site as a sub-section of the magazine, though. For an example of a magazine resource site, visit http://www.johntynes.com/rl_zines.html

SALES SITES

Sales sites are the last category of e-business. These pages are put in place to allow the company concerned to actually sell product directly to the visitors in person, rather than to encourage them to check out the company in the real world, or drive advertising links. Because the whole idea of a sales site is to get people interested in your particular product, this sort of web page does not contain banner advertising for other services (having got people to your site, you very much want to keep them there and not have them click on a banner and go to a competitor's site). Instead, web development is concentrated on making the products themselves look as attractive as possible while maintaining the greatest surfer-friendliness. Attractive layout and design are vital, but do not be tempted to include large graphic files, clever Flash animations or Java applets on main pages, because the minute or so each can take to download will have 99 per cent of potential customers turning to faster sites. Instead, use good page design to appear professional.

The other critical factor with a sales site is being able to take credit cards. We'll cover that in detail later on but, for the moment, just note that the great bulk of internet purchases take place using credit cards, and that almost no-one is prepared to make the real-world effort of printing off forms or posting cheques in order to make a Net purchase. Customers consider, perhaps rightly, that if they have to drop back into the offline world for such things, they may as well buy offline in the first place, where they can see what they are getting. There are two broad divisions in sales sites, but they do overlap considerably in many cases:

BROCHURE SALES SITES

Brochure sales sites act as a presentation showcase of available products. Potential customers are guided through to the category of item that they are interested in, and can then access detailed sales information on specific products, add that particular product to a personal virtual 'shopping trolley' (often called a 'basket'), and either continue shopping or then go to a payment page, generally credit card based with options available off it for non-carded shoppers.

The whole site should be fully searchable to provide maximum convenience. Although main pages should be quick to download – which means small image files – large, detailed product images should be available on individual web pages as an optional link for interested buyers to be able to see in detail what they are buying. Similarly, if technical specifications are an important factor of the product, these should be readily available. Products should be showcased on individual pages, with cross-product summary information also available – in short, the site should do everything possible to make sure that any information the user wants is available quickly and easily, without having to also download any information that is not wanted. Links to payment areas, search engines and the site's front page should be prominent throughout.

The key to a successful brochure

site is to minimize the viewer's inconvenience. If you can do that, you'll be well placed to make money. For an example of a brochure sales site, visit http://www.letsbuyit.com

AUDIENCE REVIEW SALES SITES

Audience review sales sites rely on public participation to provide information and value for specific entries in the sales catalogue, rather than giving exhaustive notes themselves. This sort of site deals in items that are of general public interest, such as books or videos, that are able to engage enough interest and enthusiasm on the part of surfers that they feel prepared to share their thoughts with others. Because it is difficult to legislate for public interest, audience reviews are normally made the prime feature when the content base is so huge that it would take a vast amount of work for the site managers to provide the information themselves.

Like brochure sales sites, it is important that the site be user-friendly. Some sites offer small bonuses and inducements to surfers for submitting reviews and information, but this can lead to people putting in ill-informed comments just to get the concession, so this issue needs to be treated with care. For an example of an audience review sales site, visit http://www.amazon.co.uk

As a final point, it is important to remember that many web sites contain several different types of e-business within themselves, sometimes separated into discrete areas, and sometimes rolled together into a pastiche. This is particularly effective when a tribute area or resource area is used to attract surfers to a site that also offers sales, but you'll find every plausible combination – and more besides – out there on the Net. When you have been able to match the idea that you have for your e-business with a particular type of site and, therefore, a clear image of what to do and how to get set to do it, you are bound to be a winner.

INTERNET BRANDING

The first contact that any internet user is going to have with your site is going to be its URL (commonly known as a web address, URL stands for Universal Resource Locator). Even if a user has surfed to your site or clicked on a banner advert that leads to it, the site's URL will be displayed in the browser window for all to see. That makes the address a vital opportunity to make a good first impression: your site's domain name (its web address) can tell surfers, even unsophisticated novices, a lot about your business. This means that having a good domain name is the single most important part of your internet branding.

If you already run a recognized business, then you should consider capitalizing upon your existing reputation with an appropriate domain name for your site. Customers that already know a company have been shown to be most likely to attempt that company's name as an Internet address or search engine string when trying to locate them on the web. A familiar-sounding domain name is also going to be easier for people to remember than some peculiar hybrid name that bears little or no relation to the company in question or, even worse, the sort of long internet address full of slashes that free web servers allow you to have. If your company is called DDM Direct, you want your web pages to be at http://www.ddmdirect.co.uk rather than at http://www.ddm-direct-corporate-mailing-services.co.uk and certainly not http://www.geocities.com/timessquare/10053/ddm.html...

This is particularly true if your company is associated with a successful brand or other sort of intellectual property. Current customers and/or fans will very much expect to be able to find details of the brand at web sites with

INTERNET BANKING

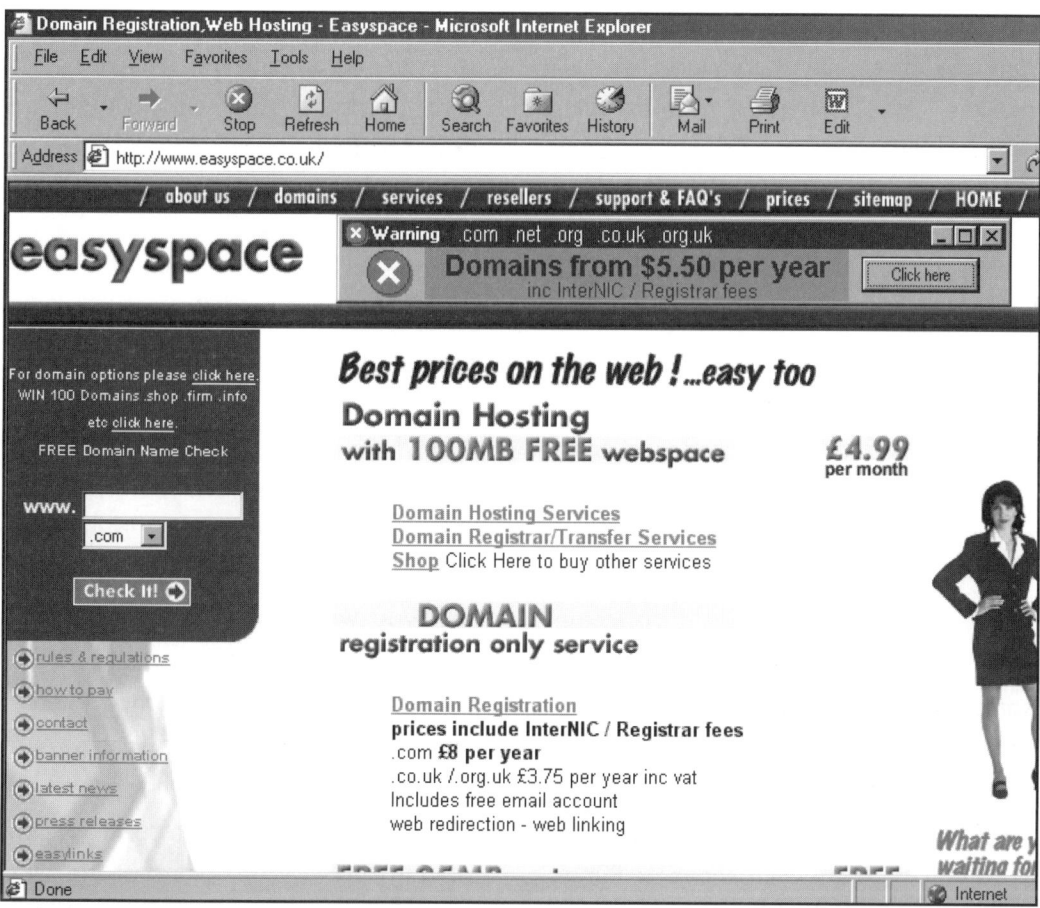

Easyspace: it sells domain names and space and it's easy!

names associated with it, and may try those as a first line of approach. Often, if you do not own those domain names, the same fans will purchase them as tribute sites, and then subsequent fans will never make it to your site at all. That means that it is critical that you control the most obvious domain names associated with your brand.

If you have the money to do so, you might want to purchase secondary and subsidiary domain names associated with the brand as well. That means not just the main name, but also close misspellings and mispunctuations, secondary features or characters, and so forth. To give you an example, imagine that Microsoft wanted to protect the online presence of their world-famous Office suite of software. As well as the most obvious names like microsoftoffice.com, they might consider subsidiary alternatives like msoffice.com, ms_office.com, microsoft_office.com, microsoftofficesuite.com and microsoft-office.com. They might also give some thought to the individual parts of the program, with domains such as microsoftword.com, microsoftexcel.com, microsoftpowerpoint.com, microsoft-access.com, microsoftoutlook.com, and even alternatives such as msword.com, microsoft-word.com and just plain word.com. Of course, you have to stop somewhere. It would be easy to quickly come up with a near-infinite list of domains surrounding even a moderately complex property and, no matter how hard you try, there will always be things that didn't occur to you. One useful thing to do, though, would be to at least purchase the .com., .co.uk and .org set that go with your brand, such as mycompany.com, mycompany.co.uk and mycompany.org. With domain name registration prices dropping all the time, this would be the lowest safe option. How far you take the protection of your brands on the Internet with the purchase of domains will have to depend on your personal inclinations and the amount of time and money at your disposal. For people on a tight budget, the most important consideration remains getting a domain that meaningfully reflects your company or brand.

REGISTERING YOUR NAME

If there's no particular existing business or brand that you want to capitalize on – or if you want to distance your e-commerce business from your traditional business set-up, because it is targetting a different market sector for example – then you will need to come up with a domain name that is available for purchase, either from the Internet domain name authorities directly, such as InterNic.com, or from one of the myriad of domain name resellers. At this point in the Net's life, almost all the good general company names have already been reserved. The bad news then is that if you do not have a specific business name to draw upon, you will probably need to go to a reseller. The good news is that about 50 per cent of the currently reserved domain names have been speculatively purchased for resale, so you should be able to find a site name that has some actual meaning behind it that relates more or less directly to the subjects or topics that your site covers.

Names such as 'booksdirect.com', 'the19thhole.com', 'ineedgames.co.uk' and 'lotteryresults.co.uk' all do an excellent job of making the site's contents perfectly clear.

LATERAL THINKING?

The alternative is to select something more or less meaningless as a domain and hope that the name you end up with manages to sound attractive to the varied ranks of Internet surfers and shoppers, but a whole raft of recent business failures suggest that this is an extremely dangerous option. Spectacular business flops like boo.com (a clothing e-store) and clickmango.com (a women's magazine site) had troubles, in part, because their names were inherently irrelevant to the great majority of shoppers. It seems that you would be better off with a site name such as iloveracing.co.uk than with a theoretically 'cooler' but inherently less meaningful name like hottapioca.com. Another mistake is to go for a site name that is too long to remember. Some few specific phrases can work well – astitchintime.com for example – but in general, long names are confusing to surfers, and make it less likely that your site will be visited. Any domain much over 16 or 17 letters in length (before the .com or .co.uk extension) should be considered with a certain amount of suspicion.

The above holds true for sales sites, but different types of site have different general specifications regarding what actually makes a site name effective. Tribute sites need a name that relates as directly as possible to the subject that is being discussed on the site. If your tribute site were about cabbages for example, then you might want to obtain a site name such as 'cabbagelovers.com' or 'brassica.co.uk'. If the site were about the rock band Queen, then all sorts of possibilities – from freddymercury.com through killerqueen.co.uk and even down to b-rhapsody.net or 7SoR.org – would be appropriate. As long as the name has a meaning that demonstrably ties in to the subject of tribute, then it will work.

Promotional sites are frequently corporate, and those should be kept as close to the business name as possible. To do anything else is to risk confusing the people you are hoping to inform. If they are showcasing a family or individual, then a domain name taken from your personal name is great if it is available, but common names like 'davesmith.com' will have long gone. You may be more lucky if your name is unusual. Failing that, personal promotional sites, even showcases of art or writing, are able to successfully use the sort of free home page address mentioned earlier. Alternatively, a name related to the subject matter of the showcase or other promotional subject can be used to great effect, if you can obtain one.

ALLURING?

Banner sites and spam sites need to have enticing domain names to lure the unsuspecting surfer into the site, and most are indeed called things like 'hotsexygirlsnaked4free.com' or 'makemoneyfast.co.uk'. With a bit of persistence, it is not difficult to think up a name of this sort that is still available. As the surfing population gets increasingly more sophisticated, though, these types of site name are starting to ring alarm bells in most people, and hit rates are falling. However, if you want to try a site of this sort, you will need to find a name for the site that promises the content you are offering (or are pretending to offer).

Resource sites, like sales sites, ought to follow the general site-naming guidelines fairly closely, but if they are particularly closely focused on one particular area of knowledge or information, you can also name them as you would a tribute site. This can be an effective strategy, if an appropriate name is available.

You also need to give a little thought to the 'extension' of your domain name – the tailpiece of the site after the first . symbol. Different domain extensions mean different things. In the UK, for example, .ac.uk indicates an academic institute, and .gov.uk indicates an official government site. Commercially, the only real options open to businesses in Britain at the current time are .com, .co.uk and .net. To start with, .net domains can be largely discounted, as they suggest to experienced web surfers that the site in question is amateurish – they are cheaper to buy from new than .com sites. That leaves .com (indicating 'company'), or .co.uk (indicating 'UK company').

The main difference is in geographical tagging. A .co.uk site is immediately identifiable as a British company, while a .com site is assumed (until proven otherwise) to be American – particularly by Americans. This means that if you want a world-wide sales presence, such as for a site that provides only free information, or that sells only subscriptions to downloadable material, .com is by far superior. However, if your main market will be domestic – in other words, if you intend to sell a physical product needing to be shipped, or to pass information to the UK business community, then a .co.uk is actually superior, because British citizens tend to feel more secure buying goods (or getting information about UK material) from a British site. Legal redress, transport and contact are all far simpler and cheaper, after all, if you buy within the same country.

Go to http://www.afternic.com to buy resellers' domain names on auction, or http://www.internic.com to try reserving your own and, either way, remember that you may not get your first choice – nor even your tenth, particularly with new reservations.

Once you have your site named, you also need to consider making sure that it follows any corporate standards for imagery, logo, colours and so on that are already associated with your business. If your company has a strong corporate identity already in place, then the only time that you might want to consider not using it on your web site would be when you were trying to keep the Internet and real-world sections of your business separate. That aside, if you look at large corporate websites such as British Telecommunications' www.bt.com or the Automobile Association's www.theaa.com, you'll find that the entire site is based on the design standards that are already associated with that group – so bt.com is largely blue, while theaa.com is black and yellow, for example.

This is even more important if you have a strong brand or intellectual property associated with your company. Popular characters need to be visualized within the site's pages in one form or another, important makes or models recognized or alluded to, even major settings or areas indicated. Different regional identities or strong brand components may even need their own sub-areas, branded appropriately from a neutral front page.

Keeping already-existing corporate branding and bringing it over to your web site is easily done – it takes little more effort than any other design scheme – as long as it is considered right at the start of the web design process.

SETTING UP YOUR E-BUSINESS

Once you've got the basics of your web site settled, there are a number of tasks involved in getting your e-business up and running that need to be dealt with before you can effectively go live. It may seem too obvious to be mentioned, but the first thing you should do is to sit down and work out whether the business that you are planning is actually viable.

BUSINESS PLANNING

There isn't the room in this book to go into full details of starting up a small business – that's an entire book in its own right – but that is how you should consider any attempt to set up an e-business web site. If you're doing anything less than fully planning your strategy, you are setting yourself up for failure. Before you do anything else, you should make sure that you have a business plan, financial projections, fully sourced funding, as well as marketing and customer research to indicate how successful your business is going to be. We'll look briefly at each of those elements, but before that there is one key question that you should be asking yourself: would your business idea make money outside of the web?

The sad fact is that an extremely high percentage of the e-businesses who fail do so because the business concept itself is poorly thought out. If the idea sounds ludicrous as a real-world proposition – 'We'll sell high-fashion shoes by mail-order catalogue', for example, fails because high-fashion customers do not buy from catalogues; they prefer to be seen in good shops and try different items for style and comfort. Therefore the venture is doomed to failure.

Before you try to set up an electronic business, take the core idea and work out how you could make it pay in the real world, without any help from the Net. If you can see a way for it to make money, then it should translate successfully to the web. Most successful web sites can be translated successfully into mail order businesses, magazine/fanzine or book ideas, games, clubs/societies, professional services or research services. Direct sale of products should always be considered a mail order business, because that is how it translates in the public mind – and that means that goods that do not sell well by mail order do not necessarily sell well online.

GETTING YOUR MESSAGE ACROSS?

The one exception to this process, of course, is if your web site is not actually supposed to make any money. It may be for purely promotional or informative purposes. In this case, the web site should be considered a marketing exercise and any expenses and investments associated with it written off against hope of later returns, just as would be the case with a magazine advert. That doesn't remove the need for the other elements of set-up and web design – the site still has to be effective and attractive, and be marketed to web users – but it does mean that you don't need to worry about whether it works as a business on its own.

Assuming that your idea does stand up as a sensible concept, you still need to spend some time examining the actual way that the business will work. The first step is to make sure that you have a detailed, effective business plan.

A business plan is a carefully structured document that sets out the details of what the business intends to achieve, by when and how, and who are the key personnel supposed to actually achieve this. This can be broken down into several sections. First of all, you need to detail exactly what the business involves – what service or product it is going to offer, how it differs from competitors, what unique benefits it has to recommend itself and, for e-businesses, exactly how it is going to generate money (will it be by paid subscription, through banner advertising or sales of goods?), and how quickly it is going to generate it.

After that, you need to work out what the costs of the business are. These include direct day-to-day financial costs, such as any wage that you may need to pay yourself in order to live, the cost of designing site upgrades, the price of computer upgrades and replacements, and the money involved in maintaining it all. However, there are also indirect costs, such as the time that the site will take you to keep it up and running, the amount of updating it will need, costs of marketing and advertising, the paperwork involved, legal requirements and responsibilities, and the time that will be required to process orders and queries. Against all of those various financial costs and obligations, you have to weigh the potential of the site to make money, and come up with a figure for how much profit the site needs to make each week in order to pay for itself. This is known as the break-even figure. You will need to work out how the break-even figure translates in terms of the way that your site will make cash – in other words, in terms of the number of subscriptions, click-thrus or sales that you will need to sell. If you think that the break-even is achievable, then you can proceed.

PLANNING AHEAD

A good business plan should also include details of where the business premises will be (after all, you'll need some sort of space for paperwork at the very least) and what staff will be

Whatever line of business you are planning to go into you will need a decent computer set-up.

involved in generating new up-to-date content, marketing and advertising to get the site known, running technical support and maintenance, and dealing with administration. If you are going to have full-time staff, their wages will need to be considered in the break-even, and you'll need to provide an office, desks, computers, equipment, telephones and insurance. If you're doing everything through contractors and freelancers, you will still need a space to keep records, invoices and payment slips, and so on. The personnel involved in the running of the site should be listed by name, with their responsibilities and track histories clearly detailed.

There will be a certain initial outlay involved in setting the site up. This includes the initial investment in site content and design, web programming, web space purchase, the initial advertising/marketing push for the site, domain name purchase, company formation if appropriate, as well as your time and money getting it all organized. This total is the amount of money that the site will have to generate on top of the break-even figure in order to become profitable. Most new businesses aim to hit profitability during the first year. Take your best guess of your turnover (the amount of money that you are expecting to get in each week – and be realistic, not optimistic), subtract your break-even figure for a week to get your weekly profit, and then divide your total outlay by your weekly profit to see how many weeks it will take for you to actually make any money from the business. If it is much more than a year, you may want to consider whether the business is actually worth the time and effort involved.

FINANCE

You will also need to make sure that you actually have enough money to pay for setting up and running the site. Most business experts suggest that you need to start off with enough money to cover your outlay and three years' worth of your break-even figure in order to cope with the ups and downs of business life. However, it's not important if the business is not to be your main stream of income and will not have employees. What you absolutely need to have is the cash to pay for the initial outlay and, what's more, to be able to consider it a gamble (as all new businesses are) and work on the basis that the money has gone for good. If you cannot afford to lose every penny of the initial outlay, then you will be in a very vulnerable position if things don't work out the way you hoped. A bank, financial institution or investor may be prepared to loan you the money for the outlay, but that requires an extremely detailed business plan, particularly in the current climate of stockmarket nervousness over the viability of Internet sites.

The final area that you will need to consider for your business plan is your target market. Are you attempting to aim your site at people who have a certain interest or have a specific requirement? On the whole, what sort of people are they? Where do they live? What is their usual financial profile and background? You have to be specific. Remember that if you are actually selling something, then you are aiming at people who buy by mail order. You may also have other specific aiming needs – if you're selling guitars on your web site, you need to aim at people who play guitar, for example. All those different qualifications have to be met by each of your target customers – so you would be looking for people who buy by mail order AND ALSO who play guitar, not people who buy by mail order OR who play guitar – so the more conditions that restrict your target customers, the fewer of them there will be. You need to be honest and realistic, because it's vitally important that you yourself know who your customers are going to be.

If you do some customer research and find that the people you are targeting are all in the lowest income brackets, you will need to make sure that your site sells lots of small, individual, cheap items or services rather than a few large ones. If your target market is rich, you will need to make sure that the site is extremely impressive, well advertised in the 'right' magazines and newspapers, and that the products are 'reassuringly' expensive. You should include as detailed a profile of your target customer as possible in your business plan, along with notes on what that sort of person likes and how you will adjust your site to reflect their personal preferences and attitudes. If you are planning to attract investment for the site, you may also need to add in information about the steps that you will be taking to market your site and its services to your target customers, including what other sites you will seek to place banner adverts with and so on.

Finally, you also need to have an idea of how you will receive money from customers. Unfortunately, it is not possible to deal in hard cash over the Net! The most popular and successful option is by direct credit card transfer. This adds a certain amount of cost to your outlay in terms of obtaining a merchant account and paying for the coding of the transfer software, but it is a lot more achievable for small businesses than it was two years ago. If you do not want to go this route, then you will have to wait for cheques to be physically posted to your business address along with order forms printed or faxed to go with them, either offering credit or delaying shipping/access until payment is cleared. Other options include insisting on personal visits so that cash can be collected, which means the customers have to be in your local area, using bank transfers (despite the inconvenience and expense to the customer of using this route), or setting up premium-rate telephone lines to pay an account through a premium call, although these tend to be specific to a given country and so hamper international trade.

Once the details of your business plan are in place and you feel confident that your business idea will generate income or otherwise prove successful, you can move on to the actual physical process of preparing for the production of your web site.

OBTAINING WEB SPACE

Once you have finalized your business plan, you will need to organize some web space. There are several options open to you. If you have a powerful computer with sufficient free disk space, a permanent connection to the Internet (via a leased line or an ADSL link), the appropriate server, mailer and DNS software if necessary, and the technical know-how to set it up, you can host your own web site without having to bother with purchasing any web space. Your Internet provider may or may not permit you to associate a domain name of your own with that space; if they do, you may have to pay a fee for that service. If you want to run a medium or large scale Web site, then you really do need to obtain the necessary equipment, leased line and (if appropriate) permanent IT support staff to run your site yourself.

If you do not have the necessary set-up, or if your Internet provider does not allow you to specify a domain name and you want to do so, you will have to find a company that can provide you with some web space. This is called web hosting, and web hosting falls into three main categories: free, tied and open.

FREE... OR IS IT?

There are a number of web sites that provide free web space accounts to any user who requires them. However, there are a certain number of restrictions that apply. First of all, you may only be able to design pages for the site using the host's own pre-prepared templates. That will mean that your options for design and content will be extremely limited. You will not be allowed to include web scripts, which will limit your ability to use forms and other interactive items. The site hosting your page may be extremely slow – most free ones are – which will frustrate users, and it will also contain banner advertising imposed by the hosting company which you are unable to alter and which you receive nothing for. Finally, you will not be able to specify your own domain or URL, and will have to make do with whatever long, cumbersome URL you are given. On the other hand, the site will be free... This sort of operation can be found at http://www.geocities.com

GETTING TIED UP

Tied web space is provided as part of a package with a dial-up Internet account. In this sort of deal, you pay a monthly fee for the ability to dial into your Internet provider and turn your machine into a mini node on the Internet. As part of this basic deal, the provider also supplies free web space (usually 10MB or so) associated with the dial-up account, hosted on their own servers. You will be able to design your own pages to host on this type of server, but you still may find that you are restricted regarding the scripts and forms that you are able to use, and may still be unable to specify your own domain/URL for the site. However, more and more dial-up providers are also offering 'business' dial-up accounts which allow the user to specify a domain, include a much greater range of scripts and media as part of the web design and, in some cases, even come with their own e-

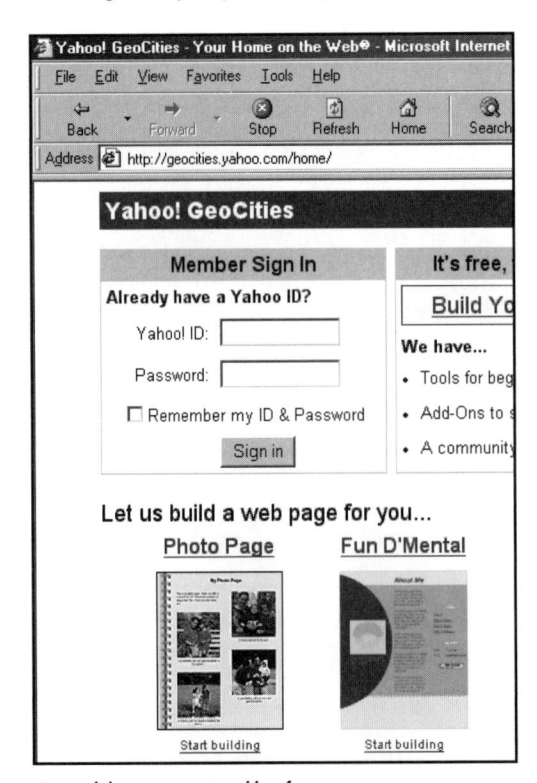

Free web hosting is not a problem for some.

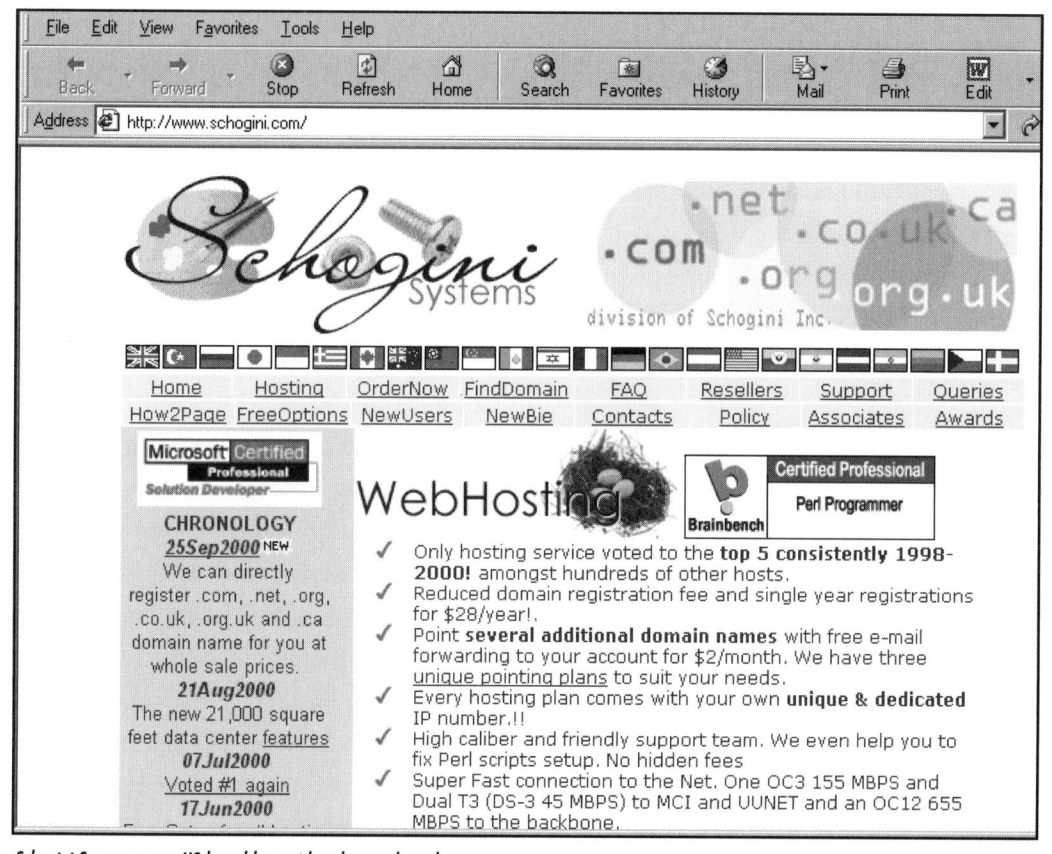

Schogini Systems are a US-based host with a deserved good reputation.

---

commerce credit card approval servers built in. For an example of this type of company, try

http://www.demon.net

THE REAL DEAL

Finally, professional web hosting sites offer open space, where you pay a fee for a certain amount of unrestricted disk space and a fairly generous amount of bandwidth. You can use any type of script, media stream or other web design element in this sort of space. You will be expected to provide your own domain name for the site to be hosted under (for details on how to buy a domain, see Chapter 14, The Domain Name Game). Mail to the domain name will be served back to you by one of a number of routes, and you will be free to set up any commerce servers and password-protection areas that you wish to. You will have to pay a higher monthly fee than you would for the other types of web space, but the service you get, and the free rein you have to do as you see fit, tend to make this the best option for most serious small sites. For an example, visit http://www.schogini.com

PREPARING CONTENT

Before any web designer – yourself included – can actually create a web site for you, you need to have prepared the content that is going to go into it. That means that you need to have the text, photographs, video clips and logos you will want to use on the site ready and available for the site designer to program together in the manner that you specify. It's not really possible to make any sensible sort of start on the site without that resource available to you. It is even good to have an idea of how you want your site to look. It can take as long, sometimes, to prepare the content as it does to actually go ahead and program the site. Most site designers will create computer graphic images for the site design as required, so you won't need to have those, and they can put in appropriate text for links and headers, but they will for the most part need everything else that you want the site to include.

If you are not yourself a professional-grade writer and your site is going to hold any original pieces of text (as opposed to forms, disclaimers, catalogue copy, corporate brochures, archaic books and/or anything else prepared in advance for a different purpose) more than about 250 words in length, then you will need to hire a professional writer. Few things are more disastrous to a web site than badly written text content. Find yourself a copywriter who is able to prepare material for use on the web and commission them to write the articles that you want to include. Most photographic imagery tends to come from catalogues or other stock, but you might also need to have some photographs taken. Again, if you are not a professional or talented amateur, then you would be best obtaining freelance assistance in assembling the images that you need.

When you have all of the original material that is going to go onto the site – photographs, logos, text files and anything else – and a rough idea of how you want it all to fit together, then you will be able to start designing the actual site itself. For an example of a UK-based professional web design company, visit http://www.geckografx.com

DESIGNING YOUR WEB SITE

Good web site design is a critical part of e-business success. Internet users are impatient, easily bored and used to feeling able to get exactly what they want as and when they want it, with minimum inconvenience. A successful site has to do everything it can to make sure that it fits with those expectations and prejudices, because otherwise very few surfers will stay around long enough to see what the place actually has to offer. The next site, after all, is always just one short click away.

The most fundamental issue to worry about is the quality of the actual programming that has gone into making the site. There are always several different ways to achieve the same end result in any computer programming operation, and that still holds true for web site design. It's an important issue; even the two main browsers, Netscape Navigator and Microsoft Internet Explorer, handle the page coding – called HTML, or HyperText Mark-up Language – in slightly different ways, taking certain parts of the HTML in different orders. That means that if the coding of the site is not precise then, even with the most basic page designs, you can have a web page that works perfectly well in Explorer but that does not display at all in Navigator – and perhaps just because of the position of one ')'.

As the site gets increasingly complicated, with frames, pop-ups, Java scripts and executables, CGI scripts, streaming video data feeds, Flash animations, secure servers, external banners, SQL database queries and all the other bits and pieces that go into making a properly professional web site nowadays, it becomes more and more critical that each part of the site is programmed properly. Without rock-solid coding, all sorts of unexpected and peculiar problems will crop up, making pages unavailable, producing broken links or causing any one of a number of strange effects – even completely crashing your surfer's computer. Needless to say, any such aggravation will have your potential customer exiting your site at high speed, never to return.

But how do you go about making sure that your site is properly programmed? Well, the first step probably lies, nowadays, in steering clear of manually typing in HTML code. In theory, all you need to write a complete web page is a text editor and a good working knowledge of HTML, but that's where all the little missing brackets and unclosed quote marks really can come into their own. If you are designing a fairly basic site – an information or tribute site, for example, rather than a sales site – that doesn't need loads of flashy add-ins and complicated server-side programming, then there are plenty of web page assembly programs that will help things work properly for you.

These programs work a little bit like desktop publishing programs or other forms of page layout software. When you start, you are presented with a blank page. You create text areas within the page, type into them, and format the text inside them just as you would with a word processor. You can drag images and other media stream types into the page, create links to other pages in your site with point 'n' click mouse work, set up frames and even layers quickly and easily, and anchor everything properly so that it all displays the way you want it to. You can build a whole site in this way on a page-by-page basis, creating all the different links and so on. If you want to do the advanced stuff, you can do that as well; good web design packages now support just about everything, as long as you have the script, query, database or stream somewhere on the disk. When you are ready, you tell the program that you want to publish the site, and it will produce all the files for you so that you can put it up on the web.

In other words, you lay out the pages, and the program takes care of all the HTML for you. These web design programs are extremely sophisticated, produce fairly good code, and can be made versatile enough to do everything you want. Some come with pre-set web page and web site templates so that, if you don't mind looking a bit 'samey', you can cut your work time down drastically. They also often have lots of walk-through tutorial files, so that you can find out how to do what you want to do if you're not particularly confident.

The best known web design programs are Microsoft's Front Page and Macromedia's Dreamweaver.

DESIGNING YOUR WEB SITE

Macromedia's Dreamweaver, one of the easiest and most comprehensive web site building programs on the market.

Which you are better off with depends on your requirements and confidence. If you're not particularly used to creating web pages and only need something basic, then Front Page is the answer. Microsoft has a well-founded – and fully deserved – reputation for nannying its users, and Front Page, like the Microsoft Office suite, is very good at helping new users do simple stuff, but a lot less good at letting advanced users do more complicated things. If you know what you're doing, then Dreamweaver is considerably better, and will greatly repay the extra effort involved in using it – but then if you need Dreamweaver, you probably already know that! In fact, Dreamweaver is complex enough that you can do pretty much any web design with it, and it is the program that the great majority of professional web page coders use.

There is a second option, however. A number of firms are releasing software designed to give you a commercial web site with the bare minimum of trouble.

These come with commerce scripts, shopping baskets, financial secure server scripting, catalogue pages and all the other elements of a full e-business site already coded – you just put in the details of your particular business, and off you go. You'll need written details and scanned pictures of each product, images of your logo/s, and a number of other standard business details ready to hand, but if you have all the information assembled, actually creating a shopping site for yourself is extremely quick. Programs like this, such as Site-In-A-Box, have met with quite a lot of enthusiasm from the smaller web businesses.

There's a downside of course. To ensure sufficient flexibility to create you a site that matches your needs, the programs have to do most of their coding in a loose, flexible manner. That means that the final web site is not as stable and well-written as something designed bespoke, and the actual file sizes of the pages themselves are often considerably larger than a professional coder's work would be. That could mean that the site is slower, prone to crash unexpectedly, may have odd results on some types of browser, and takes longer for surfers to download. If you can afford the time and/or money, proper individual coding of your web site is a better, more stable solution.

The third option, of course, is to go to a professional web site design company and commission them to create the site that you want. This is the most expensive of the three options – bespoke design from people like the Wolf Network, http://www.wolfnetwork.com a solid British firm, will cost you around £2,500 for a slick, professional web site of moderate size and complexity, although cost is always on a case-by-case basis – but the difference in quality is sharply noticeable, and you also have the option of specifying exactly what you want to a professional, who will take the site back and revise it for you if there is any misunderstanding or you change your mind about something. One big plus is that you don't need to worry too much about the company's exact physical location; everything can be done by email and telephone. You want to stay within your own country to make sure that the company designing your site understands the legal issues surrounding your e-business, and for your own protection, but apart from that, the exact location doesn't matter.

A professional web design house will also be able to generate any content for your site that you do not specifically want to produce yourself. That involves extra fees, of course, but any solid professional firm will agree to generate web copy from catalogues, brochures, corporate literature or, if you are a start-up with none of these things, from first base. There will always be data that you have to provide – your name and details if nothing else – but good web design companies will go as far as to arrange product shoots, commission writers, and even generate video streams, logos and branding for the site for you, if that is what you need.

If you go down this route, you will need to accept that no-one ever has quite as good an understanding of a business or idea as the person who created it, so you may need to be patient with the site designers if they make assumptions that do not quite fit with your own. Almost all firms will allow you to freely request revisions to a site, provided that your initial brief detailed items which have not been perfectly recreated; and all will make any new changes that they did not know about that you now require after the fact if you are prepared to pay a notional sum for the revision work. Most companies will also arrange purchase of domain name, hosting, technical support, maintenance and updating for you, if you need these services.

Whether you are specifying a site design for a professional firm or producing the pages yourself in Dreamweaver, there are a number of issues that you need to bear in mind. The most important is user boredom. It is always difficult to look at something that you have created or commissioned and think for a moment that there might be anything wrong with it, but if you are going to make the most of your web site's impact, you will want it to be as appealing and useful to visitors as possible. Unfortunately, that means having to accept that web users are immensely impatient.

It's bad enough in the USA, where local-rate calls are free, but in the UK, where home surfers have to pay local phone charges by the minute, everyone is extremely reluctant to waste time and money downloading large files and web pages. Given the congestion on the web nowadays, it can take up to a minute to download a 100k file from a busy web site – and 100k is not very much space, really. There are several things that you should keep in mind when designing your site. Pictures take up a lot of download time. Small buttons and plain logos aren't too bad, but large graphic images or, worse, chunky movie or sound files, can take minutes to download sometimes, and that will prove to be disastrous.

Try to make sure that picture files on your main pages – the welcome page, any search pages, general index pages and so on – are each no larger than 25k, that they come to no more than 100k in total, and that there's no more than 16 files per page. The page code itself, the HTML for the page, should be kept to a maximum of 50k if possible, and ideally trimmed down to 20k or so. When you put your site up, go to a cybercafe, visit it from there, and time how long it takes your first page to open. Less than 10 seconds is fantastic, under 20 is acceptable, but more than 45 seconds and you'll lose all but your most dedicated visitors.

The key lies in splitting the site up into small bite-sized chunks where possible. Each page should download quickly and painlessly. If you need to get across larger pieces of information – a long text file such as a report or book, an Adobe Acrobat form (a job application form, maybe), a music file, an executable program, a large picture, or a movie – then they should always be available through optional download links that the visitor should click on, rather than built into the page. Have them available together from a download page, or cluster images together in a thumbnail gallery, or otherwise make sure that the users don't find themselves stuck downloading a huge range of data that they might not want. Nothing is more certain to generate bad feeling.

If you have a range of products or a long list of individual items, prepare a catalogue of individual web pages with each item on one page, and an index page giving categories and brief descriptions. If you have a gallery, break it into sections however you see fit, but keep it small. If you have a database, try to make sure that you provide a script for searching it, rather than forcing people to download the whole thing. Extra information and explanation can be encoded into optional Javascript 'help' buttons by items, rather than cluttering every page with instructions that may be redundant after the first or second visit. In short, do everything you can to make sure that your site downloads as quickly as possible. Remember the cybercafe test – your personal machine may download the site many, many times faster than a web user will, because of the way that browsers store commonly visited sites. Don't assume that, just because it's fast for you, it will be fast for others. If certain items are unavoidably large – full product catalogues, detailed technical photographs, copies of the accredited standard English word list and so on – that's fine; just remember to put a warning by the link letting surfers know how big the page they are jumping to is going to be.

Less of an issue nowadays is the technical complexity of the web site. When the web was in the process of taking off a couple of years ago, the sophistication of the graphics and programming that could be put into a web site was actually far in advance of the coping limit of most home machines. Irritated surfers would spend minutes downloading a large, technically excellent page only to have their machine slow to a snail's crawl, or even crash entirely. Fancy graphic effects often just hampered users with limited graphics cards in their machines, or with a small amount of RAM. Recently, the average specification of machines has risen to the point where it can cope with any page small enough to download realistically, so you don't need to worry so much. However, you need to be aware that each extra technical innovation you include in your web site is going to cut out a certain percentage of your possible audience. If you produce a site with a Macromedia Flash opening sequence, layered Javascript frame navigation, Shockwave animations, scrolling Java indexes and machine identifiers, complicated CGI page references and content encoded into a Realplayer stream, you may find that only 50 per cent of the people who get to your site are going to be able to stay to see your content. Still, that's better than the 10 per cent that it would have been two years ago.

The final thing to think about is intrusiveness. Many web users resent things that interfere with the browsing experience and interrupt them, and a surprisingly high percentage are nervously twitchy about their personal privacy. Now that junk email – spam – is such a persistent aggravation, people dislike having to give their email address to web sites in fear of getting more of the stuff.

User registrations require people to give some personal information – at least an email address – in return for a unique username and password that will identify them to the site. In theory, this allows the site to remember the user's preferences and details, making their surfing more enjoyable. In practice, many sites use it as a way of getting hold of an email address in return for little or no added value. Some areas or functions of the site may be restricted to only registered users, but this is almost always as a marketing ploy rather than because of any genuine technical or convenience issue. Voluntary registration is less invasive, so will irritate fewer potential customers, but will also attract the interest of only a small percentage of the site visitors.

Site memberships function in exactly the same way, but with one critical difference – the membership has to be paid for, and the user expects exclusive member access to the great bulk of the material on the web site in return for their payment. In this instance, enforced login is considered perfectly acceptable, because it is protecting the surfer's financial investment. Commercially sold membership information should not be used for marketing purposes – if someone has paid for a site membership, then they will want to visit the site to get value for money, and promotions and other marketing information should be detailed on the site itself.

A more subtle way of gathering information from site users is through the strategic use of counters and cookies. Initially, web counters just recorded the number of times that a page was downloaded, but they have become more sophisticated. Up-to-date web server software can not only track the number of hits, it can identify which Internet address each page is being downloaded to, working out the number of different individuals visiting the site. By adding certain scripted queries into the background of the page, it is possible to capture the email address of each visitor to your site and build up a database of potentially interested customers that way. Cookies, on the other hand, sit on the surfer's computer and give details of what sites they have visited, when they were last there, what they did there, and so on. These allow for some interesting analysis. Even if you only have access to cookies placed by your own site, you can still get a profile of what areas of your site the user visits and how regularly, to allow you to tailor the site more closely to their needs. Some computers have cookies disabled, but this takes a bit of advanced web browser knowledge, so the majority of users don't even know that the option exists – and may not even have heard of cookies at all.

A web site can be as complicated an affair as you wish it to be, coding-wise. The trick is to never let the technical side of a web site take over its functionality or its design. A huge array of extra features can be added to your site, but ask yourself first if you really need them and if they are going to hinder the easy navigation of your site.

In summary, the web is a very competitive area and you will need to make site visitors feel as positive about your site as you can. Good web design is absolutely critical to achieving this. If you can couple good design with a user-friendly ethos, you will be able to make your site a pleasant, useful place for surfers to visit – and that means they'll come back. Getting as many hits as possible is what e-business is all about, because all commercial sales work is a numbers game: the more people you approach, the more sales you make.

This is what the insides of a web document look like...

WEB STRATEGIES

If you're going to have any chance of making money out of the Internet, you need to make sure that your strategy for generating cash is tied to the type of site you are running. It's no good trying to fly in the face of accepted convention as a sales tool, unfortunately. It never has been. A number of different patterns have arisen on the web surrounding the different ways of making money, and you're going to have to work with them rather than against them.

That means you need to have a clear idea about which type of web site you are running. As we discussed earlier, web sites fall into several broad categories – tribute, promotional, banner, resource and sales. Each has different conventions.

Tribute and promotional sites are not expected to make money directly, and you should not try to squeeze any cash out of them over the Internet. Tribute sites are considered by surfers to be the results of a labour of love. Anything you do to break that impression is going to sink the site like a lead balloon. That means that overt advertising and sales pitches are out. The only acceptable banner adverts are ones that are imposed by the webspace providers for free web accounts. You can't use enforced registrations or membership logins. You can get away with offering people a voluntary sign-up to a semi-regular email newsletter or email discussion list, but that's about it. Cookies and hit counters are acceptable, but mainly because they are largely invisible to the surfer. That doesn't mean that tribute sites are commercially useless, though. They can be an extremely good front for a related site of a different type, adding a useful bank of material and information that can draw surfers in to you. By having a welcome page for the tribute area of your site and a further welcome page for the other areas of the site, you can gently encourage people to visit the rest of the site, and move out of the tribute area, converting a surfer into a useful prospect. This sort of 'added value' tribute site can provide an excellent way of making people come back to your main site in order to refer to your information or check updates.

Promotional sites are a slightly different thing. The whole point of them is to provide information about your real-world activities with an eye to encouraging old and new clients to make use of your services or products. As such, even the banner ads imposed by free web space vendors will hamper and dilute your message. Promotional sites should be as impressive as possible from the first moment without being intrusive or having slow download times, so you will want to start with a small, punchy page. By making biographical or corporate information (as appropriate) available via the site menus, you encourage people to get in touch with you. You can also include links for the visitor to click on to email you from each page, so as to reinforce the idea. Counters and cookies are acceptable again, but only if – and because – they are hidden from the user. You will need to make sure that all the information you want people to see about you or your company is available and as easy to get to as possible. If you have a bank of info, it should be searchable; products should include photos (clickable rather than built into the page) and full technical specifications wherever appropriate, as well as easily readable reviews, summaries or overviews. Track records in the form of financial performance data, CVs or other historical information will help sales too. As soon as you make any attempt to get cash directly from the Internet community via a promotional site, you are sabotaging it fatally. Its sole purpose is to encourage people to make real-world commissions or purchases.

Visitors to banner sites know they can expect a certain amount of invasive content and slow service. Most people know how minuscule a pittance one click-thru returns, and accept that the site will have been put together cheaply and hosted on inexpensive servers. In addition, the presence of advertising banners – which are notoriously slow to download, because they are stored directly on the advertiser's site and not the banner site itself – is understood as an integral part of the service. There is a limit to the amount of ads people can take, though. You should try and make sure that the absolute maximum number of banners on any individual page on the site is just five; any more and visitors will feel that you are taking liberties. In fact, sticking to just two or three can be better. You also need to accept that in return for suffering the indignities of downloading all those banners and putting up with the slowness of the site, the visitor will expect to find good content. If you are hosting image galleries, for example, you cannot really get away with less than ten pictures in any one thumbnail gallery, although you would be able to put the full five banners there to accompany them. The images, though, should just be files, so they download easily, and not stuck on individual pages (which make it harder to save the image to disk) with more ads. You have to give your visitors something to make up for the fact that you're throwing all this advertising at them. If they feel goodwill towards you because of your content and user-friendliness, they are far more likely to click on a banner for you. You should also try to update the site every day or every other day if at all possible, and make your update policy clear on your welcome page. This will encourage visitors to come back to you, to check out your new content.

Resource sites have several options open to them. If the resource is difficult to find elsewhere, extensive, or otherwise unusually popular or impressive, then enforced registration or even membership is a perfectly acceptable route. You will need to provide free tasters of the material or facilities available inside and give full details of the benefits of signing up, but you can keep the majority of the site's content and functionality out of the way. If you don't choose to have paid memberships, then a certain amount of banner advertising is expected. This should be far less dense than for banner sites – just one banner a page – but as the advertisers are generally of better quality than banner site advertisers, the daily return is not all that different. You can also use resource sites to sell appropriate goods, bolting a small electronic store onto the main resource area. Finally, you can also approach companies for sponsorship and feature prominent sponsors' logos/banners. As long as the resource you are offering is valuable, you will have a fair degree of leeway to use different methods of commercially exploiting your site.

Sales sites, finally, are by their nature designed to persuade visitors to part with their money. The implication of that

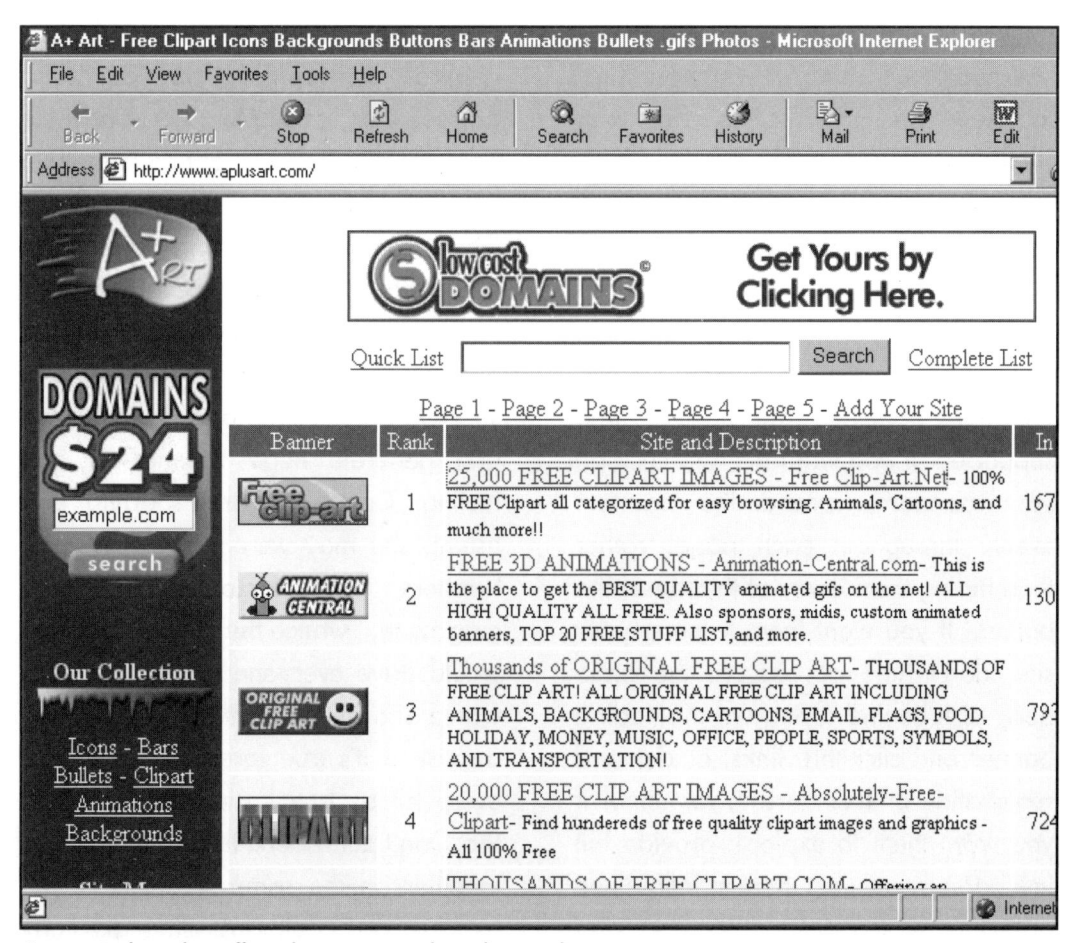

Resource sites have a lot to offer, and some manage to do it with taste and restraint.

is that surfers already feel that the whole site is a piece of advertising, and any other extraneous attempts to make money from the site will just cause problems. If people are visiting your site with a view to giving you money, they won't want to find themselves faced with any banner advertising or enforced registrations. It would be like having to pay a fee to enter a shop on the high street – utterly unthinkable. If you are running a sales site, strictly avoid the temptation of trying any extra ways to make money, and let your sales catalogue speak for itself.

Whatever strategy you choose for making money from your site, you need to make things as easy as possible for visitors to your site to do the things you need them to do. If you want them to view the information on your promotional pages, make the site clearly navigable, ensure the information is well written and presented, check that it looks good and reads easily on a number of different monitors, and include thorough site maps and Frequently Asked Questions pages so that the user feels supported. If you want them to click on your banners, spread the banners evenly throughout each page, rather than hiding them away at the top or the bottom. If you want them to enter your site, don't hide or obscure the main body of it behind a page of misleading banner and click-thru links, or demand registration or membership for entry. If you want them to explore, provide full link bars; if you want them to follow one particular route, make other links and sections harder to find. Everything that you can do to make sure that visitors do what you want them to because it is the easiest, most convenient choice will pay you back great dividends in increased revenue streams.

Similarly, you also need to avoid alienating or offending your target market. That means knowing the sorts of people that will want to make use of your site and the facilities or goods it offers, and having an idea of their general sensibilities, opinions and biases. For example, pornographic advertising banners might be entirely in keeping with a warez resource site, where your target audience is going to be young adult males who are already immersed in the subculture of the web, but cause a site dedicated to the sale of sporting and fishing goods to fail utterly and generate huge volumes of bad feeling. Conversely, the sporting and fishing site may very successfully offer banners for *Horse and Hound* magazine, while the same banners would drive everyone away from your warez site in amazement and amused disgust. If it's true for advertising, it is every bit as true for editorial content, too. Don't put widely disparate materials together on the same site, and if you express any opinions or make any comments as the site owner, make absolutely sure that they pander to the opinions and prejudices of the people who you are hoping will make you some money.

As a final point of strategy, give some thought to updating your web site. If it is a tribute or sales site holding a body of static information – historical matters, a fixed catalogue or scientific facts, for example -- there's not much that you can do to keep that material current. Everything else, however, can and should be updated as regularly as possible, and even factual material that does not change can still be added to. You can always branch into an interesting, relevant side topic on another page in your site. Without updates, you provide no real reason for a visitor to come back to your site, and return business is always easier to maintain and more commercially valuable than generating completely new business every time. That means you should think about how you are going to keep your site fresh and up to date, and how often you are going to do it.

Your update period will really depend on the time and money you have available to invest in your site. Ideally, you would update your site with new material every day. This can involve replacing older material that has a one-off "download it and be done with it" utility, like pictures, or stuff that has gone out of date, like old versions of shareware programs once the new version has been released. It can also include adding completely new material, providing interesting topical commentary or information, or expanding the information or resources available in already established areas of the site. Failing daily updates, a commercial site – banner, resource or sales – should really be updated weekly at the very least, just to keep everything current and make sure that all the material on it is fresh and tempting to returning viewers. Make sure as well that all the external links you may have in your site are still valid and won't cause an error 404 (the one your browser gives you when you request a web page that isn't available). Tribute and promotional sites are historically rarely updated, but then they are there to provide information rather than to garner huge hit rates. Sales sites may only have a very limited update provided, but it is important that visitors consider all the information on the site to be bang up to date, particularly regarding stock, prices, technical information and shipping details. Update as often as you possibly can – it will be worth it and will keep your site looking nice and fresh.

DELIVERING CUSTOMER SERVICE

Good customer service is an essential part of any business. If you can impress your customers with the service that you offer, then they will recommend you to their friends, use you again, and generally work with you to make your business successful. This sort of word-of-mouth advertising is one of the most critical factors in the performance of a commercial enterprise, and it can make the difference between spectacular success and dismal failure. If you take the time and effort to make sure that your customer service is as good as you can make it, you will generate a lot of business through the goodwill that this produces. It's well worth it.

Of course, customer service on the Internet means something rather different from the older, more traditional types of service. After all, your customers are not going to be dealing face to face with counter staff and sales assistants, or speaking to your representatives on the telephone. Given that you may not ever come into any direct contact with the customer, how are you going to impress them with the level of service that you are able to offer?

The answer, of course, is that you try to make sure that your customers' experience of doing business with you is as convenient and pleasant as possible – that's what all customer service is about when you get down to it. There are a range of different things that you can do on the Internet to deliver good customer service, and the more that you can complete, the better you'll do.

CREDIT CARDS

With the way that Internet business is developing and the increasing degree of confidence that consumers have in security and anti-fraud measures, one of the most critical customer service issues is having the ability to accept payment online by credit card. When Internet businesses first started springing up, there was a great deal of suspicion towards typing your credit card details into a web browser. That has totally changed, however. Now a lot of people have entirely positive first-hand experience of shopping online with a credit card, and even those people who have not done so all know several others who have, with no ill effects. The public has a greater understanding about how Internet fraud works, and it's not by intercepting your details online.

In fact, most of the time you have no real way of knowing what is happening to your credit card details. Even in shops where your card is swiped, the details are still printed on the roll of sales receipts, where they could be later extracted. In restaurants, the waiter will take your card away for several minutes, usually completely out of your line of sight. Not only can the details be noted down, the entire card can in fact be copied with a magnetic card duplicator, easily available for just a couple of thousand pounds. Garages, hotels, bars, even phoneline ordering services all provide plenty of opportunity for your card details to be swiped. By comparison, hacking into a secure Internet server is extremely difficult.

The real problem with Internet fraud does not come from stolen details at all. The trouble lies with CCG programs – otherwise known as credit-card generators. These tricky little programs are freely available to the hacker community and will generate a random, but nevertheless valid, credit card number, along with the name of the bank that would have issued it, its expiry date, a plausible holder's name and address and any other details that the fraudster might need. Many of these valid numbers are not actual accounts, so the bank itself has to pay for the fraud. Some, however, just so happen to be real credit card numbers of real people. When these are used, the bill goes to the person whose card it is – and another horror story of huge, unexpected bills arises.

New safeguards have made it all a lot more difficult. Most web sites and Internet businesses now require that the delivery address specified on the order is the same as the billing address of the card user, and both have to match up with bank files before the card purchase can be authorised. That means that even if a fraudster could get a correct card number and address, the purchases he made would have to be delivered to the card owner – who would be surprised, no doubt, but who is protected by statutory legislation to allow him a two-week period to return the goods for a full refund. In other words, it is no longer a good route for fraud, it is just an irritating practical joke. The few web sites that will still accept different billing and delivery addresses are coming under increased pressure to change their practices.

All this means that credit cards are becoming increasingly important for commercial web sites. The majority of Internet purchases are made by credit or debit card, and being able to process card orders online is one of the things that distinguishes an unreliable, amateurish site from a professional one in the eyes of the buying public. Originally, you needed a merchant account with a bank to be able to take credit cards at all, which meant two years of prior accounts, large fees and all manner of paperwork, so only the largest businesses were able to deal with them. However, credit card facilities are now increasingly becoming available without full merchant accounts from resellers, risk vendors and Internet Service Providers, so there is little excuse any more for not being able to process card orders.

SITE MAPS

No matter how hard you try to cover every angle, it is never possible to allow for all the different ways that people think and categorize. However you organise the information on your site, there are going to be times when a visitor is going to have trouble finding a certain item or piece of info that they are after. When you only have a small site, that's no problem; anyone can find their way around five or six pages with just a little persistence. If your site is large, though, it can be a far greater issue.

As an example, consider your company's physical address. If you have a contact details page (and we'll talk about that in a moment), then it will probably be available there – but what if you do not? A physical address could quite reasonably be on an order form page, as part of the instructions for people who do not have a credit card and want to post in an order form with a physical cheque or banker's draft. It could be in a page of corporate information, along with financial reports and trading history. It could be in an 'About X' page, nestling in with an overview of the business. It could be associated with a page of opening hours and other related items. In fact, it could be tucked into a bit of free space just about anywhere.

This potential for confusion and misunderstanding gets considerably greater when the data the user is looking for is less easily categorized than a simple company address. If you are faced with a site with 20 galleries of abstract pictures, it might take half an hour to search through it to find a specific image. The answer to this problem is to implement a full site map – a full list of links to the individual pages of your site and their contents, on one web page. Make sure that the site map is well signposted from your main pages too, because it rather spoils the effect if no-one can find it!

If your site is particularly complicated, you might want to think about investing in a fully searchable database of the site's contents, known as a Search Page. This will let people do a word-by-word trawl of the site for a specific term or phrase that they are looking for. It's expected as standard on information resource sites and large sales sites, but any site with a large amount of textual information or a particularly wide range of items would benefit from one.

FAQs

FAQ stands for Frequently Asked Questions, which is itself the answer to one of the most common FAQ questions! A FAQ is a list of common and/or obvious questions about a specific item, topic or issue, along with full answers. The idea is that if anyone has any problems or queries regarding the items or terms of service on your site, the chances are that they will be able to get all the answers that they need by turning to the FAQ.

These documents appear as a list of questions, each followed by their respective answers. In most cases, the list of questions is also summarized at the top of the document for quick reference. Particularly long FAQs – and some of them can be in excess of 60 pages long, such as documents prepared on the Internet's Usenet News service – may be broken into sections, to speed up download time. Some FAQs are structured so that there is one index page of questions, and then each answer is on a separate web page, but this is often a poor idea, as most people who use an FAQ have an interest in the answers of more than one question, and like to browse through the document a bit more extensively.

A typical FAQ might include entries as follows:

Q 12. How do I place a credit card order?

A 12. There are three different ways that you can place a card order with us. The first is to use our secure server and order over the net. Click on this link - https://www.bogussiteX.com/sales/form.shtml - to go to our order page, type in your details, and click 'authorise'. In about 30 seconds, we'll confirm your order. If you don't want to order over the net, you can telephone on 212 555 6666 and leave your order on our answering service. Finally, you can print out one of our order forms and mail it back to us here - click http://www.bogussiteX.com/sales/mail.html - for the form and our address.

Q13. How safe is it to use my credit card over the net?

A13. Our server uses special encryption to make sure that only we can see the details of your card. Anyone 'hacking' into the data as it went from your computer to ours would see only gibberish. Your card is as safe as if you drove into Manhattan and handed it over to us in person. Possibly safer, in fact.

And so on. When compiling an FAQ for your site, try to think up as many questions as you can that anyone might plausibly want the answer to. It might help you to visit a few similar sites of other people's and have a look at the kind of questions they are answering on their own FAQs. Try and be as complete as possible, and don't attempt to be evasive or defensive. Every question someone gets a satisfactory answer for from your FAQ is one more step towards a satisfied customer.

ENQUIRIES AND RESPONSE TIMES

There are always going to be queries that you didn't anticipate, or people who don't take the time to look through the FAQ. You still need to deliver first-class customer service to them, and that means having some provision for dealing with enquiries. The best way to do this is to set up a customer services, technical support or query page that provides a form for people to type their questions into and have them emailed over to you, along with that person's contact details to allow you to get back to them.

If your site is complex or covers a wide variety of areas, you might want to have different topics to choose from on the enquiry form presented as a drop-down list, so that you know the subject of the question, or so that the machine can route that particular query to the appropriate person. You could even make allowance for the user to specify their home region or country, so that if legal issues are involved in the question or if you have staff in a number of countries, you can get the query dealt with as smoothly as possible. In situations where there are going to be some details of the user's that you will definitely need to answer the majority of questions – details of the user's computer set-up, for example – then you should include sections on the form with tick-boxes for the user to select from in order to help ensure that you get the information you need quickly.

Once you have a query from a customer or site visitor, you should attempt to get it answered as quickly as possible. People are generally prepared to wait 24 hours for an answer in order to make allowances for the possibility of differences in working times – if you receive a query at 2am your time, you probably won't even see it for several hours. If it's going to be anything more than that, you ought really to email the person, acknowledge their query, and tell them that you will get an answer to them as swiftly as you can, setting a realistic expectation for when that will be. There is never really any excuse for taking more than three or four days for answering a query. It will look unimpressive to your inquirer no matter what the reason, and will work against you in the long run. If you're so swamped with customer service queries that it's impacting your workload, you need to look at revising or adding to your FAQ (or making it more prominent on your site), or hiring some dedicated customer service staff to deal with customer issues for you.

FEEDBACK AND CONTACT ADDRESSES

Feedback forms are closely related to enquiries. They have much the same structure, providing the user with an

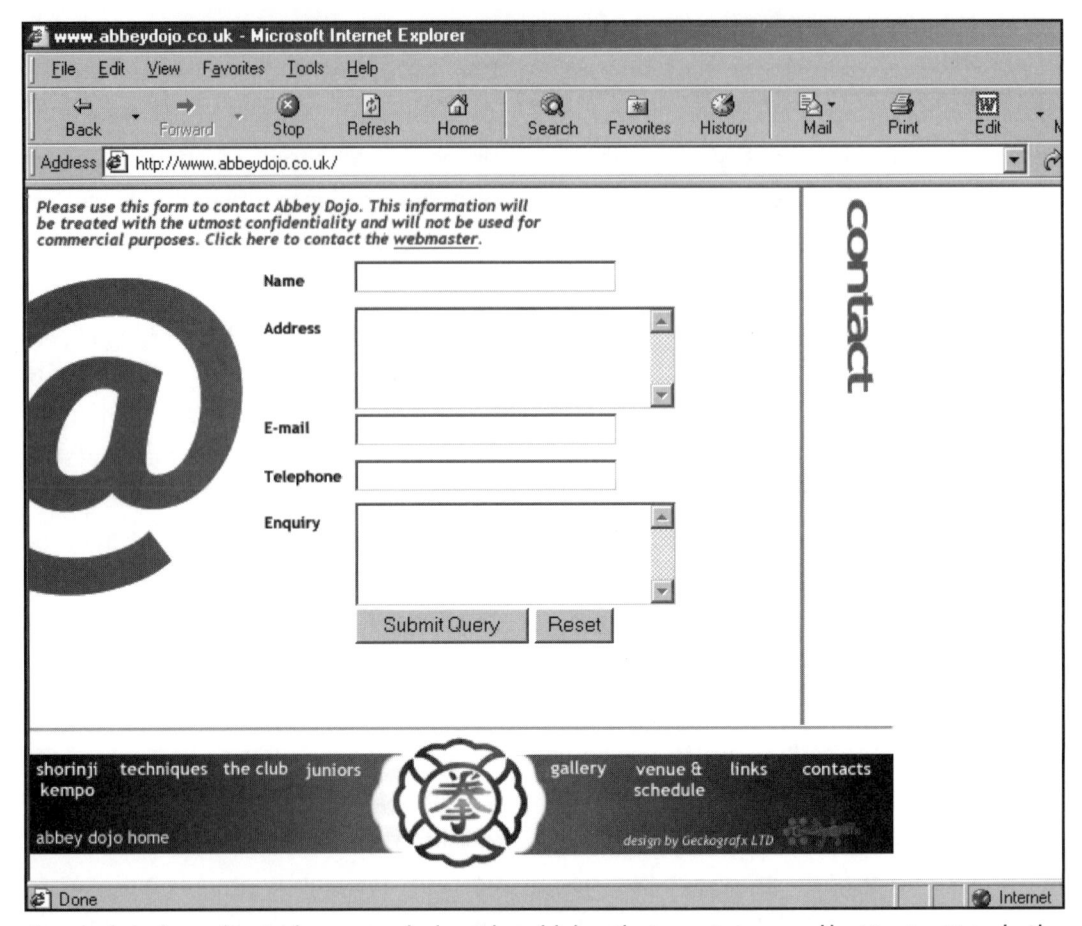

Every site, be it a huge multi-national company or a local martial arts club, has at least one contact page, used by visitors to get in touch with the people in charge.

opportunity to pass a message back to you from the pre-set web page without having to open their email program or note down addresses. The nature of feedback is such that people don't really expect an answer to their comments, so there's little time required in dealing with the material. Good practice would be to at least acknowledge comments and thank people for taking the time to share their thoughts on the site with you, but it's not necessarily that important. Proper complaints, when they are received – and you can't please everyone – should always get some sort of reply attempting to resolve the issue. People will tend to use feedback pages when they are available to make complaint comments, so there's no specific need to make allowance for them directly.

As with enquiry pages, you may find that it makes things quicker and easier for you if you include a list of topics or subject areas for the user to choose from when they are making their feedback comment, but it will rarely be necessary to ask for details of equipment or other particulars. In fact, you can even point out that the user's email address is a voluntary addition to the comment – people who are being critical may feel more comfortable if they are anonymous.

It is genuinely important to get feedback from users, particularly critical feedback. People have a lot of different expectations and strange ideas, and some are just unpleasant for the hell of it, but if a number of different people all raise the same issue, it may be something that you want to consider looking at. There's no real point trying to make changes based on one piece of negative feedback unless it points out something so glaringly wrong that you can't believe you didn't spot it before – anything less, and you'll find that you're spending your entire time chasing between pillar and post trying to please the most recent objector. Enduring or repetitive comments, though, might – and only might – indicate an area that you need to reconsider. Apart from that, have faith in your personal vision.

Along with feedback forms, you should always provide physical contact information. Potential customers are always reassured to see that there is a real person at the other end of a web site, and having your address and a telephone contact point will help to reassure them that if something goes wrong or gets complicated, there is someone that they can speak to. It'll make a big difference. You don't have to make a song and dance about your physical contact details – unless it's a promotional site, of course – but they should be there for reference should anyone want them.

TIMELY DELIVERY

When someone orders something from you on the Internet, it is important to get it to them with all due haste. Many people are still nervous about all mail order and they get increasingly anxious as time goes by. You have to remember that many people do not know anything about the Internet and therefore are pretty suspicious about the whole business. The quicker you can get their goods to them, the more fondly they will remember you next time and the 'It worked once, it will work again' factor will come into play. A lot of customers will simply come back to your site simply because one transaction has been successful and they feel confident in giving the whole thing another go.

For electronic goods, such as site memberships, information files, passwords and so on, you should have your site set up so that the item is dispatched to the recipient as soon as the payment is authorized. That means that if they are paying by credit card over your site, they should get their file, password or whatever emailed to them within 120 seconds.

Where the transfer can still be made electronically but is not set up to be handled automatically – say, for example, that you personally have to authorize emailed credit card details and then email a file back to the person manually – then you should make sure to complete the deal within 90 minutes, assuming that the order is received in business hours. You should also make it clear on the order page that the completion will take this length of time, and specify not only which hours of business you keep, but what the current local time is. This will allow people to make an informed judgement of how long it will be before they get their goods, and stop them bombarding you with threatening or panicky emails.

If the goods are physical, then you should make sure that they are received within the statutory 28 days at the very latest, but if you are generally able to make next-day deliveries (for example by first-class post within the same country) then you should attempt to do so. You can always include information to that effect on your site, so people will be able to expect rapid delivery, and be more inclined to purchase from you.

Little things such as the facility to leave a personal message with your parcel, if it is intended to be a present, or maybe a birthday parcel wrapping service might induce customers to choose you rather than your competitor. Think about the costs and if they are not too high, why not invest in some delicately advertised gift cards or packaging? This can make all the difference.

PROMOTING YOUR WEB SITE

Now you have a site, you'll want people to visit it and that's unlikely to happen spontaneously – it's going to take some effort on your part to promote your site so that people are aware of it and feel inclined to surf by. In essence, if you consider your web site to be a product, then you need to engage in some marketing – and that subject is a book in itself. However, we can look at a few methods of driving traffic to your site to start you thinking in the right way.

BANNER ADVERTISING

One of the most common ways of promoting a web site is to buy a banner on someone else's site which, when clicked on, takes people straight to your site. It's obvious why this is so successful – the people who see the banner are only one click away from your site. They don't need to try and remember your address, or find a pen to write it down, so they're more inclined to visit on the off-chance.

The first thing you need to do is to design your banner. There are strict standards for the size of a banner – 468 pixels wide by 60 pixels high – and the format in which it's saved – CompuServe's GIF format (.gif). You can create your banner using any software which can write GIF files – Adobe Photoshop or Microsoft Paint are two common packages used, although the professional web designer's choice is usually Macromedia Fireworks. Try not to make your banner too complicated – remember, it must catch people's attention and lead them to click, so simple and striking is best.

Now you must get your banner out there. There are three ways of doing this

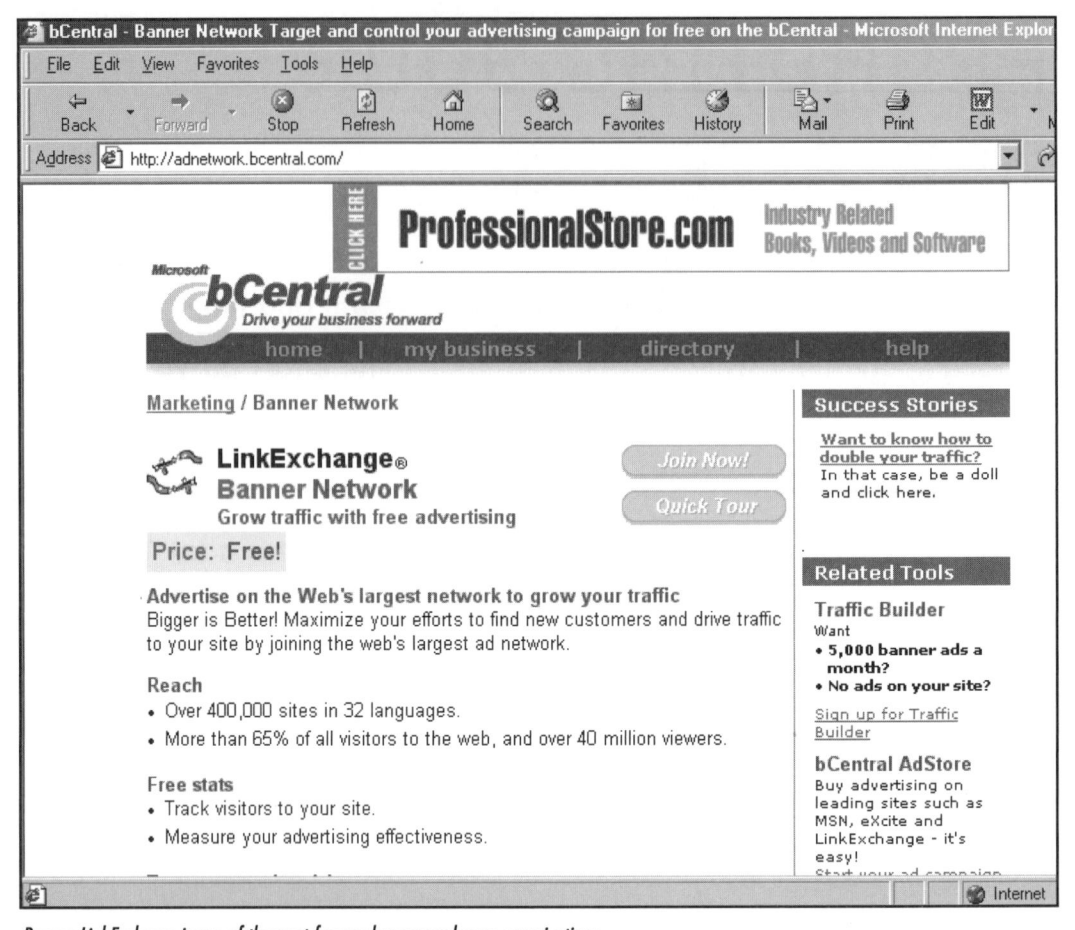

Banner LinkExchange is one of the most famous banner exchange organizations.

– new media buying companies, link exchanges and individual arrangements.

A new media buying company specializes in placing your banners on different sites. They charge per *impression* – a measure of the number of times your banner is seen, dependent on how well targeted the placement is. At the time of going to press you can expect to pay between £10 and £50 CPM ('Cost per mil/thousand' impressions). A media buying company may also offer you a rate based on the number of click-thrus – the number of times people click onto your banner and arrive at your site. A good media buying company to start taking a look at can be found at http://www.doubleclick.com.

Link exchanges offer you a reciprocal arrangement – you host banners on your site which advertise other sites belonging to the exchange, and they in turn host banners for your site. Link exchanges may charge a nominal subscription charge to join their service, and will suggest the level of click-thrus you may experience, but by the very nature of the exchange arrangement, it's more difficult to guarantee visits this way. Visit http://www.linkexchange.com for a good starting point.

Finally, if there's a site which you feel attracts a lot of visitors who may be interested in your site – maybe they're covering the same sort of information, or are targeted at the same audience you are – you may be able to approach them directly and either buy banner space on their site or suggest a mutually beneficial reciprocal agreement.

EMAIL

Another way to tell people about your site is to use email. With the advent of HTML-based email messages, now commonly supported by most major email packages, it's easy to put a hyperlink into an email, offering the recipient the same convenient one-click access to your site that makes banner ads so popular. And because email is sent directly to someone, rather than a banner which waits for people to come across it, email marketing is a far more proactive method of driving site traffic. It's cheap to send emails (though bulk mailings may swamp a small-to-medium-sized Internet set-up and so you may want to pay a professional mailing company, which costs a little more than doing it yourself) and the cost-per-response rate is minuscule compared with most other forms of direct marketing.

First though, a warning – unsolicited email is known as *spam* and is widely regarded as a nuisance on the Internet. As of the time of going to press, it's not illegal to email anyone (so long as the content of your mail doesn't contravene any decency, blasphemy or other laws) but you may well find you receive a large number of irate replies from people who just don't appreciate what you've done. See the section in this chapter on usenet for more about the retribution foisted upon spammers, and some suggestions for minimizing it.

Now that's out of the way, there are two main things you need to carry out a successful emailing campaign – an email, and a list of target addresses.

The number of people who visit your site will directly repay the effort you put into crafting the email you send. Of course, a number of people will always click on a link in an email just out of curiosity, but you can have a far more effective response by spending a little time considering what you want to say and writing it well. The subject line is important – many people choose whether to read a mail or delete it immediately based on what they see in the headers. Don't lie in the subject line, don't use all capital letters and try to use a professional-sounding name in the From field. With all of the facilities modern word processing packages offer, there's no excuse for bad spelling or grammar. Make sure that the body of your message is brief and to the point – people didn't ask for your mail so the least you can do is waste as little of their time as possible!

Lists of email addresses can be bought from list brokers for a relatively small cost, or you can get a list broker to send your mails for you for a little more. Alternatively, you can get software from various repositories on the Internet which will grab addresses from Usenets, the web and other sources, and make your own list. Either way, remember that it will be untargeted and many of the addresses won't be current, so don't expect miracles. That said, a well-written email campaign can return very satisfying results.

EMAIL LISTS AND LIST SPONSORSHIP

Email lists (or *mailing lists*) are subject-specific (generally) and their face to the outside world is merely a single email address. The thing is, when one message is sent to that address, it gets replicated and a copy sent to every person who's subscribed to that list. They are often used by manufacturers to communicate information about their product ('a closed list' – only certain people can send mails to the list) or by groups of like-minded people discussing a certain subject ('an open list' – anyone subscribed to the list can send a mail which everyone else will receive). There are also *ultra-open* lists, where you don't even need to be a subscriber to send a mail to the list, but these are becoming difficult to find, due in part to their misuse by people trying to promote their web sites!

An email list is a far more focused target for an email extolling the virtues of your web site and imploring people to come visit than a randomly mailed message, but people on lists also tend to be more protective of the sense of community that such a form of communication engenders and are likely to act negatively if thoughtlessly spammed. It is also very easy for the owner of the list to remove your subscription and ban you from re-subscribing, and as you must subscribe with a valid email address, it is easier to be tracked down.

With all that said, though, a well constructed and thoughtful email in a list entirely suited to its subject, or where you are an active participant, would most likely be well received and would be quite likely to drive traffic to your site.

Another way of using mailing lists to your advantage when promoting your web site is to sponsor the list. Certain list owners will take payment in return for adding a short commercial message (such as may draw people to your web site) to the bottom of each message sent out to the list. Because you've arranged this with the list owner, people very rarely complain about the intrusion, and also because they know you've paid, recipients are far more likely to accept it as a credible piece of promotion.

Most mailing lists are reasonably small though – the most massive maybe numbering a thousand recipients – so while being highly targeted, only a small number of people will see your message.

USENET

Millions of articles a day pass through Usenet, a lesser-trodden area of the Internet which still attracts hundreds of thousands of readers a day, all over the world. Usenet is broken down into thousands of newsgroups, covering an incredibly broad range of subjects, and it's those divisions that make Usenet attractive to spammers – it's far easier to target a message advertising your site toward people who may actually be interested in its contents. And because Usenet is a notice-board, where messages are posted for people to come along and read, a single message posted to the right board can be seen by more of your target audience than a thousand randomly sent emails.

Getting onto Usenet is simple – your ISP should run a Usenet news server so a quick call to them should give you the address of that. Both Microsoft Internet Explorer and Netscape Navigator allow you to read Usenet by plugging that address into the relevant configuration setting, and if you'd prefer to use a stand-alone application, News Express and Turnpike are very good options.

Once onto Usenet, picking the right newsgroup or newsgroups is complicated only by their number – there were 30,000 at the last count! They're broadly divided into computing, business, recreational and alternative hierarchies, and amongst those subdivided and subdivided until an individual group is reached. Pick carefully though, as people who read Usenet are more picky and more reactive than email users and a spammed message in the wrong group will result in hundreds of mails appearing in your mailbox.

The advice given for emails is also valid on Usenet though – take some time to write a good message, avoiding spelling mistakes, all capital letters and promises of turning visitors to your site into instant millionaires.

Most Usenet programs would allow you to try almost anything in the Return-To and From fields that get added to your article when it's posted and this may initially look like a good way of avoiding recriminating emails – have them directed to some non-existent email address. But depending on the contents of your site, and particularly if you're looking to carry out business transactions with the people who visit it, fake return addresses can affect your credibility, making people less inclined to come and have a look at your site in the first place. And any competent Usenet regular could track your message through headers which you have no control over if they were annoyed enough, anyhow. Some ISPs react badly to complaints of spamming made to them about their customers and may, in extreme cases, terminate your Internet access, so careful planning and a respectful approach are a far better option in the long run. That said, see the later section on guerrilla marketing for ideas which may be less than acceptable to many members of the public, but are guaranteed to make an impression!

TRADITIONAL MEDIA

So far, all of the methods that we've looked at for driving traffic to your site have been Internet-based themselves, but we mustn't forget that it's quite possible to use traditional media and conventional marketing practice to increase your site traffic. This method is relatively more costly than using new media solutions, but what it loses financially, it gains in credibility and accuracy. On the Internet, it's still very difficult to target a specific audience – web sites still know very little about the people who look at them, and while a web site about car engines is likely to attract a good number of mechanics, this is still difficult to prove from a marketing point of view. Traditional media, on the other hand, have an incredible strong and detailed understanding of their audience. Media buying companies, who specialise in placing adverts in the right magazines to reach a certain consumer, are experts on human nature and the behaviour of every type of person. So if your web site proposition is valuable and you really want the right people to see it, a traditional media campaign may well be worth the extra cost.

This book couldn't possibly got into all the detail required to plan and execute a successful traditional media campaign, but we can cover the basics quickly here.

You must know your audience – who do you want to visit your site? What things are they interested in? Is there an obvious magazine or newspaper which they would read? Do they even read papers and magazines, or would it better for you to target them using radio, television, or even bus and taxi-sides?

Understanding your audience will also help you develop the advert that's going to speak to them. Again, like the email message, it must be short and snappy, but do you want to use humour, or fear, or coercion, or association to grab their attention? Is your advert going to be factual, or a teaser? The only obligation, during the design of the ads is to make sure that the your web site's address is obvious and readable.

If your Internet business is big enough, you may want to engage an advertising agency to handle your campaign. We are talking big bucks here, but the investment may well pay off, so it's definitely something to consider.

And if you can't afford an agency, or even a quarter-page ad in the *Andover Advertiser*, consider using classified ads to get your web address in front of people. If you can write well, or if you employed a professional author to write the content of your site and can get him to write a classified ad, a snappy 30 word ad in the right category could get just the people to log on to your web site that you've been after all along.

Remember, with advertising, it's the unusual that people tend to notice, so think about putting your web address where people don't expect to see it – on T-shirts (which you could initially give to your friends, and then sell on the site as an extra revenue stream), or fly-posters, or anywhere else your imagination can conceive. Be creative and a traditional media campaign could turn your web site into a household brand name. Which is what you want really, isn't it?

GUERRILLA MARKETING

Guerrilla marketing (and its sanitized, corporate version, viral marketing) is effectively all about using creativity and non-conventional means to create word-of-mouth in order to promote your web site. It's all about starting a buzz, about getting your message heard where it wouldn't normally be, and is often considered outside the edges of any promotional campaign. But it can be extremely successful.

Viral marketing involves producing a message so *sticky* that consumers keep it around (such as a useful freebie, or exceptional piece of merchandising), or producing a message so engaging that consumers propagate it using their own resources. For instance, a common method of viral marketing currently is to produce a small animation which carries your web address. Making it funny, disgusting or entertaining in another way almost guarantees people will copy it and email copies to all their friends and workmates – all the more people to see your address and maybe visit your site. Of course, the most engaging messages are always messages of gloom and doom, so a controversial rumour, started by you, which, while not ultimately damaging to your business, entices people to check out your site to find out more, will probably drive an exceedingly large number of visitors to your site. Remember, though, that rumour is short-lived. Your site needs to retain people's interest once you have them there.

One of the easiest ways of starting a rumour is to post an article on Usenet posing as a client of your company (or even a competitor, or an excited first-time user), giving yourself the opportunity to say things that people would automatically discount if they knew your connection with the site in question. Or, alternatively, you could use IRC (live chat), or web chats for a similar purpose – sometimes the anonymity afforded by the Internet can be very useful. Again, ask your ISP about IRC (or go to http://www.mirc.com). Once logged onto an IRC server, you'll find all manner of discussions going on in channels which occasionally have meaningful names. With some clever subterfuge, the people in the right channel may be fertile soil for you to plant the first seeds of your guerrilla campaign.

Do keep in mind that guerrilla marketing can always backfire on you. It's not a mainstream practice, and while it can produce great results for little financial investment, people are always looking out for someone to slip up and there is every possibility of your credibility and ultimately your reputation being permanently damaged by a guerrilla marketing stunt gone wrong.

SELLING ADVERTISING SPACE AND EMAIL ADDRESSES

Before you can go about trying to make some money from your database of Internet users, you need to actually compile one, so that you have some information that you can sell. There are several methods of building a customer database, each one of them with its own particular bonuses. As well as considering the type of database you wish to use and what you're going to store in it, it is also worth considering the various tricks and tools that you can employ to make the database more efficient – and therefore more valuable.

BUILDING A CUSTOMER DATABASE

To start with, it is important that you spend some time thinking about what you want your database to contain. Most customer databases contain the name and email address of the client in question, as well as the details required to contact them.

There are a number of types of information that can be added to this. They are not strictly speaking essential, but can be added to the records (a record is one line of a database; the information about one client) to give the database user a greater understanding of that individual. These extra bits of information can include details of what the person has bought, how they have paid, and how often they have purchased things. These often feature in client databases, together with the standard payment terms that customer has been offered, and their credit limits on that site, if any. You should note that while each of these items adds to the knowledge provided about any given customer at any one time – and hence is more valuable to a purchaser – it also adds quite a lot to the size and complexity of the database being used, and therefore makes it more of a headache for you to use in your day-to-day running of the site. There are a number of things you can do with the database at the site admin level, though, to make your own personal use of the database a bit easier.

The first step to making your site database more effective is to use Cookies. These are electronic 'tags' that are sent from your web site to the user's browser, and they will remain on that person's disk drive until intentionally deleted or until they expire (generally in 40 year's time!). Your web site can be set up to register if a cookie from your site is in the person's machine and, if so, it can be programmed to adjust what the site comes up with according to their preferences, habits and interests. Some browsers can be set up not to accept cookies, but that will have no real negative effect on the user's experience. The web site can also be set up to register the impact of multiple cookies, so that people who return to the web site on a regular basis can be given 'fast track' results to what they want. The only real alternative method of keeping track of customers while they are at the site itself – as an option for those people who do not want to use cookies – is to implement a registration system. This takes a bit longer, and does put quite a lot of people off, but is more reliable in the long term. Of course, your site probably doesn't need to 'manage' its users much, so cookieless people should provide little problem.

In addition to cookies and registrations, you can also get user email addresses through 'harvesting'. With this method, you provide certain tempting files for the user to download via FTP, or the Internet's File Transfer Protocol. The standard requirement for FTP is that the user's email address form the password that the web browser submits to gain access to the file – and from there, you can take a copy of it. While the person is downloading their file, you're receiving their email details. Similar query requests can be built into the actual web pages of your site, so that opening a specific page prompts the browser to send the user's password to the site. Finally, you can also run opt-in email lists on topics relevant to the site, and then extract email addresses this way.

You should of course bear in mind that the provisions of the Data Protection Act make it illegal to electronically hold any information about a person without their knowledge and consent, so always ensure that people understand that you will be obtaining their email address.

SELLING THE DATA

There are a number of very different opinions on the whole issue of the sale of personal data. They broadly divide into people selling data, who say it's fine, and people whose data is being sold, who dislike the fact. Most people do not like thinking that their information and details are being sent on to others without their specific prior consent. It feels like an invasion of privacy that you are not yet aware of. However, you should bear in mind that the sale of information for use of marketing database companies can be an extremely lucrative venture. Indeed, many businesses have been established and run for several years on the simple trade of information for money. If you're looking for a marketing list broker who deals in email lists, try G-Tec on http://www.gtec.co.uk

It's a cliché, but there really is no knowledge that cannot be translated into money and/or power by one means or another. What must be considered, as always, is whether or not the prospective gains outweigh the costs. On the one side, information brokers will often pay well for the right data at the right time. On the other hand, people who do not know that their information is being given out will often be (at the least) somewhat upset, maybe becoming angered by the distribution of something that they consider to be personal and private. While you may get some cash for your database of customers, you may also find that receiving that money costs you dearly in client goodwill and repeat sales if it becomes obvious that you are selling data.

The best way around such problems is to give the customer the choice of whether or not you are allowed to pass their information on. At the point where they enter their details, put a small box at the bottom of the page that allows the customer to indicate whether or not they will consent to allow you to sell their information. If they will not allow it, just ask them to click the box. In this way, the customer recognizes the fact that you are putting their needs first, and your own gains second. This is always a good thing.

There are people who will distribute personal marketing information without the permission of the user. Indeed, some

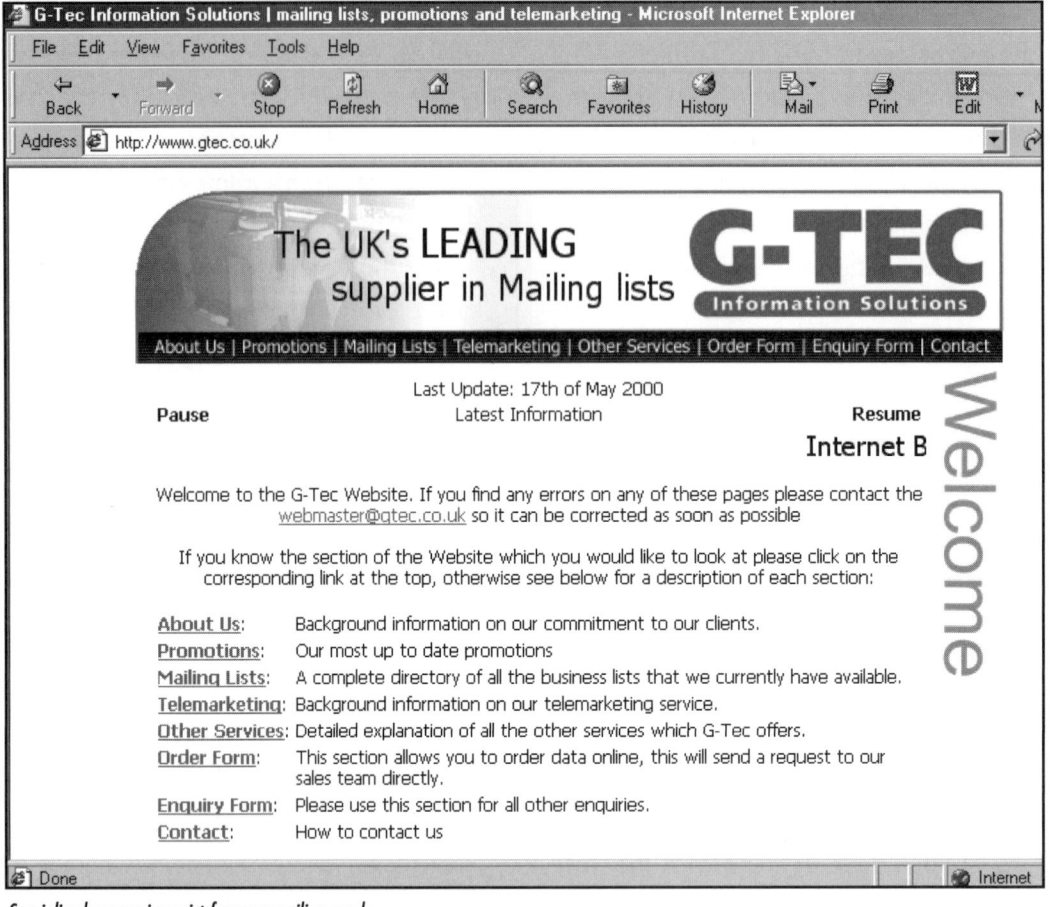

Specialized companies exist for your mailing needs.

of them will even distribute the information without the permission of the database owner! These people sometimes fall foul of large lawsuits, but even if they escape legal action, nothing good ever came of deceiving the client base you are trying to establish. Companies like this swiftly develop a reputation as untrustworthy. Would you buy anything from someone you didn't think you could trust with even your name?

ADVERTISING AND SPONSORSHIP

Quite apart from your client list, your site can be a valuable billboard for others to purchase space upon. There are several different types of advertising that can be obtained, and each of them has its own little implications, both positive and negative.

Non-click web advertising is typically sold on a 'cost per thousand impressions' basis, or CPM. An 'impression' occurs when a visitor to a web site views a page where an ad is displayed, whether the user actually clicks on the banner or not. Whenever a page is "served" to a user's computer screen, special measurement software counts the impression.

CPM advertising is amongst the least well paid of the advertising methods, with rates varying from £2 to £10 per thousand impressions. Consumers will have to be visiting the site on a massive basis – the millions of hits a week that a free porn site can obtain, for example – for this form of advertising to pay off in any great volume – and CPM advertisers don't like to be placed on porn sites, as it's often offensive to their core client base. On the plus side, the advertising is fairly easy to get hold of, and there are not many requirements placed on the host web site.

The primary form of external sponsorship (as opposed to advertising) comes through the form of sales-only banners. These are adverts on your web page that activate when a particular item that you are advertising for another company or web site is sold. Information about the sale and your part in it is relayed back to the person who supplied the item. Upon receipt of this data, the supplier sends the agreed sum of money to you, the owner of the web site. There are no real drawbacks to this form of banner sponsorship other than the fact that the fee will only be paid on certain products, and not on all the items that are being sold. Also, depending on the supplier of the sponsorship, the sponsor may want to take some space on the web site promoting the product – ie, your site.

Another form of advertising comes in the form of click banners. These are items on the web page that serve as a link to the advertiser's web site. Referring clicks from your site are counted and analyzed for sales made to people you referred, to give a click-thru advertising figure, which provides a ratio between the number of clicks on a particular banner and the amount of sales done. This shows your performance, and the amount you earn per sale may vary depending on how impressive your ratio is. Click-thru advertisers often only pay on a commission basis, with the amount of sales referred from a particular site equating directly to the amounts of sponsorship paid for the advertising.

Another form of advertising is CPC (cost per click) advertising. This pays based on the number of times that a particular banner is clicked upon. It is not highly paid, averaging 2p–5p per click on a banner. It is to be noted that in sufficient number, these banners can generate a reasonable amount of revenue, but they do risk swamping your site with click-on advertising, irritating surfers. It is also a fact that many people do not spend time clicking on banners, so this form of advertising is only for those who know that they're going to get the required high volume of people looking at the site.

DTC (direct to consumer) advertising is gaining strength, with the main thrust of it being directed at the general public rather than the business world. Such things as radio, TV and billboard advertising are covered by this. A smaller form of this advertising that you might be able to make use of is to place advertisements for your site in smaller shops and centres, exchanging real-world advertising space for online advertising space for the people whose space you are using. Many shops take a mildly sceptical view of this, but the number of people who want to advertise on the Net – and have no idea how to go about it – is growing. Given the difficulty of gaining the support of larger corporations, it is often worth looking at smaller shops, maybe even concentrating in certain regions, to see if they are willing to advertise your services in their shops. In return, you can place an advert for them on the Net. This type of sponsorship often works as a mutual partnership type of thing, with each company using the other as a holding post till they can branch out into that direction themselves.

The final form of advertising is in the form of pop-up banners. These activate when the user selects a certain option or link, and open in a new window. The user has no automatic control over these items, they just appear. This form of advertising is often the cause of much frustration for users. What tends to happen is that the new page will open along with four others, swamping the user in unwanted pop-ups. Only spam sites tend to use this sort of advertising. The person whose site is being sponsored will pay a set fee for each month that the auto-activated banners are on the site, and also they will often pay a fee if a certain number of hits is achieved over that time period. The drawback, of course, is that many people automatically close such 'unsolicited' banners without looking at them, so the advertisers very rarely get the advertising that they are looking for, and at the same time the site is slowed down by the need for the user's browser to download the advertisements as well. In other words, everyone loses.

To keep track of the success that a particular form of advertising on your site is having, it is necessary to have some type of counter installed into the site. Every time the site is visited, or a graphic on the page is activated, the page will register a hit. These are totalled at the end of the day and sent back to the main database, where the site owner and the owners of the various banners can evaluate how things are going. This is not a good way of monitoring the amount of traffic to a particular site, as clients often go through the pages, see what they are after, and then click on that before the remainder of the site downloads. Once again, cookies are used in these matters, making sure that if the client bounces back between the pages five or six time in the course of their browsing, they will only register the one hit unless the cookie is no longer present in the cache.

Another method of using cookies to help with the hit verification is to set the cookie to be date specific. This allows the user of the banner to look at the rate and frequency with which that particular user is going to sites. It also lets you see where the user is visiting most, where they are going least, and – together with the enquiry database and product database – find out what the user actually wants, letting you plan an effective strategy from there.

To find advertising, and people willing to sponsor your web site, can paradoxically be simultaneously easy and difficult. Firstly you have to identify what it is that you are providing, and then you have to narrow down who is providing you with the type of product you are selling. In certain web sectors, there is very little advertising to be obtained. These sites are typically the high-street stores, and the products that they sell. It is often futile and unrewarding to seek sponsorship from these people, as they will have their own web sites that promote their goods far more than you could.

A primary method of finding advertising is to hunt across the web sites of competitors with sites similar to your own, and see what sort of advertising they have on their sites. It is likely that such advertising will be available to anyone who asks for it. Very rarely is such advertising limited and, in the cases where it is, the costs of getting the advertising very often outweighs the benefit of having it. Each company which provides advertising will have someone who is responsible for their advertising strategy, and dealing with the financial aspects of having you host their advertisements.

All of the major companies who provide advertising will require some sort of business plan to be made available, outlining what you intend to do with the site. This plan should contain the information necessary to allow your potential advertisers to make an informed choice as to whether or not they should support you. You should have very definite ideas on what you are prepared to allow them as space on your web site, as many of the sponsors will want exclusive advertising in a large portion of a smaller business' web site. A good option is often to give them an entire section within the web site, detailing only their products. Many of the larger sponsors respond well to this sort of incentive. However, your business plan must also be sound. Of the thousands of people every year who approach any company for sponsorship, maybe 10 per cent will actually get it.

The best way of obtaining advertising from one of the larger companies is to visit their web site and search it for the people who deal with Internet advertising. Most of the larger companies have a small section of their page devoted to the people who are most in demand. One of these people will be the e-marketing manager. This will be the person who deals with new prospects, and it will be their team that goes through the proposal that you send. Nothing impresses people less than a proposal that is sent to the wrong person — it suggests that guesswork has played a large part in the presentation of the proposal, and therefore that guesswork may also feature in the actual proposal, casting rather nasty doubt upon the finished thing. Far better to know at all times who you are talking to and why, rather than asking to be put through to the relevant person and hoping to get it right.

There are some companies on the web that will provide help in securing advertising. Some of these provide free information to people who want to keep up with current developments, and while the information offered will not be presented as quickly as some pay-per-report services, they are a good starting point to see how the advertising trade as a whole has been moving. For an example of a site like this, go to http://www.internetnews.com

In summary, it is easy to secure advertising from people. It is not the advertising that is the problem, it is making sure that the advertising that you

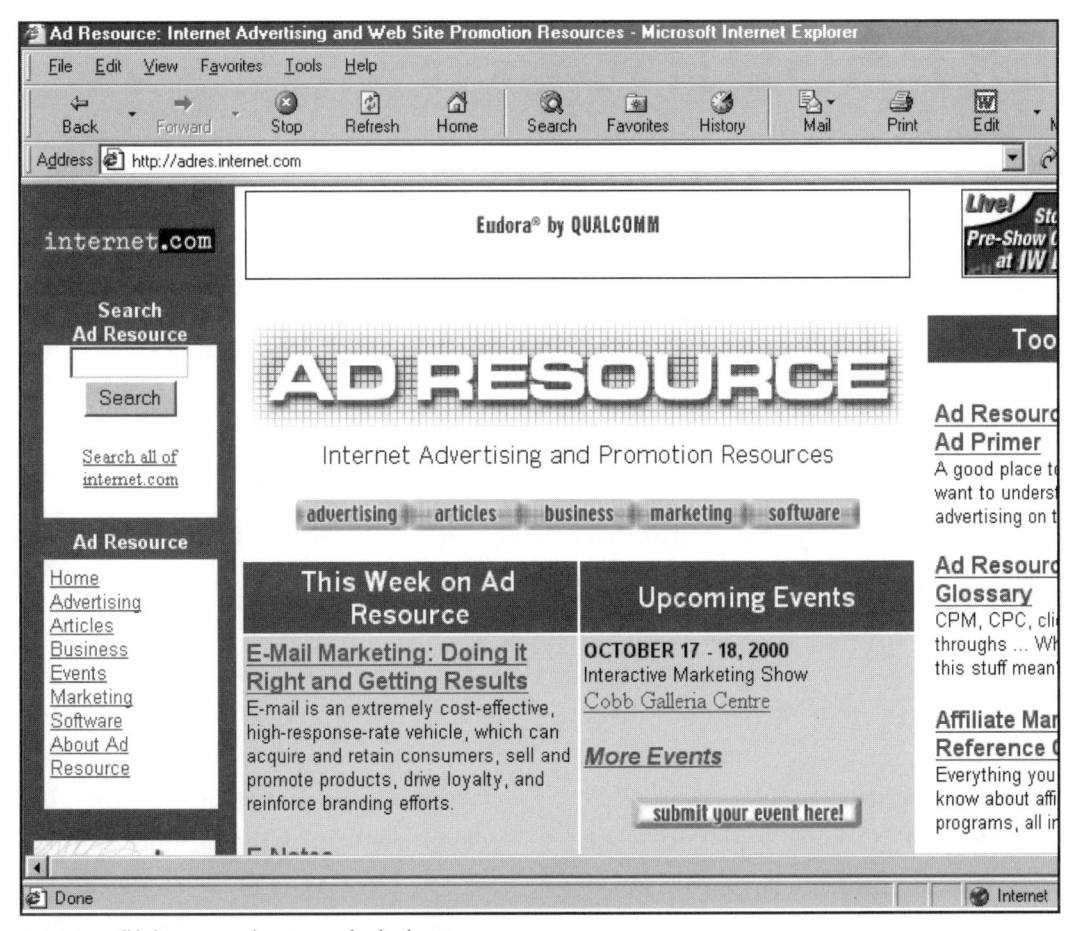

Some sites will help you grasp the concepts of web advertising.

get is the right sort for you and your site, and that it will pay you what it promises. Young companies would be advised to start out with CPC and DTC advertising, as these will often yield the best results for the work that goes into them. Larger companies will be able to make use of direct sales banners and click-through schedules. For more details on the nature of advertising and how to get hold of it, visit http://adres.internet.com/

Advertising is a powerful and unavoidable way to get people to know you exist. Remember that in the Internet, you exist along with over two billion other web pages (the accepted figure for January 2000), so it is essential that you should make sure that you stand out.

EXPANDING YOUR BUSINESS

If everything goes according to plan, then the time will come when your web business is doing well, returning decent profit levels and gathering plenty of hits. That is the time to start thinking about expanding the business, reinvesting some of the profits in order to increase your potential to earn greater amounts. There are a number of things you can do at that point in order to expand.

If you consider a traditional retail business as a model, three routes of business expansion become fairly plain. A shop that is doing well and wants to grow can either purchase larger premises and expand its range of goods, keep the first shop as is and open a second shop, starting a chain, or (more rarely) sell a franchise of its business to other people in return for a certain ongoing cut or purchasing arrangement. All three of these traditional methods of expansion translate readily onto the web.

Larger premises means expanding your web site. In this model, you create new subsections of the site and add them into the general umbrella of the overall site. These should be related to the current site as much as possible, but without duplicating the material that you already have on offer. Look for closely-related subject areas or activities that you can exploit. Sales products should be things that are of interest to your target market – if you sell fishing equipment, you could add a section of all-weather clothing, for example. Alternatively, you could add sections of your site that fall into a different category of web business – such as a resource area if you are running a successful sales site – and bolt it on the side of your existing site. It will help attract further interest, and may open up entirely new revenue streams for you as well, so it can pay off in both ways.

Of course, whatever you do, you must apply the principles that worked for the first part of your Web venture to the expanding part. There is no point in having created a wonderful site just to spoil it with extra pages that don't relate at all to the previous ones, or which clash with the rest of the design. You must also be confident that you can actually provide the service you are going to advertise now: if you do add a page about all-weather clothing, you must have a list of all-weather clothing retailers available, with good deals and clear profit/cost figures etc.

It is not in the scope of this book, however, to show the various strategies behind a successful business operation on a large scale – strategies such as expanding laterally, cornering a market or things like that. It is well worth talking to your accountant, financial adviser or bank manager if you think you have what it takes to create an empire. They will be able to steer you in the right direction and give you advice in what kind of area to invest in once your venture is on its way to the top.

Opening a second shop means diversifying your web interests by creating a second, independent web site. This can be a simple parallel to your current site, doing much the same thing for much the same people but with a slightly different slant – this is the way that most banner sites expand; adding a redheads site next to a blondes site, for example – or it can be a radically different proposition alltogether. In general, there are advantages to staying at least within the same target market. That way, you can use both sites to cross-promote to each other (possibly even using guerrilla marketing), which will always be advantageous unless your target market is so small that you would end up competing with yourself. On the other hand, if you have another good idea for a totally different site then provided it works, you will be spreading your interests across a wider area, and lessening your risk if the market shifts a bit sometimes.

Most people, however, find that when they have set up all the people and systems to work within one market sector, it is a far greater effort to start up in a different sector, because you're back to square one. If you stay in your home sector, you're usually half-way there already. As an example, any successful site will be requiring regular updates. If you have any editorial content on your site whatsoever, that means that you will need to be writing material – or hiring writers to do so – based on your current market interests and issues, and your knowledge will be up to date in that area. If you switch to a new area, you may need to find new writers, or spend some time researching the cutting edge of the topics and issues in the new area.

Finally, selling a franchise involves

A good way to show the various ways in which your business expands is to show the different areas it is involved in and update your demo page regularly.

persuading other people to set up versions of your web site – in different countries perhaps, or on slightly different topics. The reason for them to pay you money for this rather than to just go and do something similar is usually that your business is well-known to people, and so it already has a name and reputation that will help make it successful. Less commonly, you can offer all the set-up, branding, graphics and goods for the franchise site (based on your own) to the purchaser, greatly reducing the effort that they have to put into starting up, in return for paying you a wedge of cash. Franchising, though, is most successful when you have created a strong brand through marketing that other people will recognise as being of good market value.

Another advantage of having a franchisable brand is the potential to sell merchandise based on your site's brand. When you have a name that people recognize, you gain the potential to produce and sell novelty items based on the site's name and/or design – things like T-shirts, coffee mugs, mouse mats, baseball caps and so on. The items need to look good if you're going to sell them, of course, and they have to follow current trends (particularly for clothing), but they can be a surprisingly good source of income if you have some snappy images or effective designs. They also have the benefit of acting as free advertising for your site, reinforcing the strength of the brand. Typically, this sort of item is available for franchisees of yours to purchase from you at less than retail cost (but still at a profit to you) to also sell from their own site.

So much, then, for the real-world model. There are also things you can do to expand your web business that have less obvious correspondence to the physical world. One of the most obvious steps is to increase the update rate of your site. No matter how often you update your site, you can always increase that rate. Even if you're already updating with material on a constant basis, you can still increase the volume of material you add or change at any one time. If your site doesn't have anything much that could be updated, the material on it may still be open to expansion, by adding new items, details, information, files or whatever. If you are feeling wealthy, you might like to take on a new permanent member of staff simply in order to increase the update volume.

Fresh content always encourages people to come back to your site – although keeping old content available as archives is a good thing, if you have the server space for it. People who like your site will want to see as much of its content as they can, and if they have to miss a couple of update periods for one reason or another, they will be grateful for being able to catch up on the stuff they missed when they get back from whatever it was that was keeping them busy. This type of expansion roughly equates to a magazine shifting from monthly publication to fortnightly, or to a daily newspaper increasing its number of pages.

Another option is to invest in superior technology. If you aren't running your site from a dedicated server that you own, running on a cutting-edge computer with maxed-out memory and processor speed connected to the web via a permanent T3 connection, then there is room for improving the speed of your site. Investment in top-grade technology may not really pay off if your site is still small, but at the very least you can give some thought to moving to a better (ie, faster and therefore more expensive) web hosting service, or getting yourself greater bandwidth and/or server space.

There are a lot of options open to you and be aware that, as far as connecting to the Net is concerned, you can barter. There are a number of communication companies out there who want your money and your custom, so you can shop around to be sure to get what you need at the lowest price. The world of communication is moving extremely fast, so make sure as well that you keep abreast of the recent technical developments in this field so that you don't get flogged an old low-speed phone line when digital data transfer is available in your area.

At lower levels, the cost of the improvement will be well outweighed by the benefits of providing a better service. Free web space, in particular, is worth every penny you pay for it – ie, not much at all – and the extremely slow page performance that you usually get from these services, coupled with the extensive advertising banners they impose on you, make them unpopular with surfers. It's well worth the £10 a month or so to get up to the next level of web hosting. Similarly, once you're at the lowest levels of paid hosting, it'll usually be worth upgrading to better services as soon as you feel that the site will justify the improvement. Banner sites are an exception, of course; their content usually means that only certain hosting services will support them, and each individual page usually makes little enough that it's necessary to stick to cheap or free services. This sort of expansion is something like a real-world company upgrading its corporate infrastructure.

A third choice is to move to a better domain name. Better, in this particular case, usually means shorter, snappier and/or more apt for your business. The chances are that you will have to pay someone to purchase an already-registered domain name from them. You may even want to attempt to persuade an existing web business to part with their current domain name, although this is difficult. Moving from a low-grade domain name like 'fishingstuffforsale.net' to a high-grade name such as 'flyfishing.com' could cost you a lot of money, but it will also go a long way towards increasing your hit rate and your status and profile. You also need to bear in mind your existing customers, though. If you have a client base, you will not want to miss out on their business. The answer is to keep the old site on as a shell and use it to redirect people on to your new site. You can set this up to happen automatically. At the same time, you should remind them to make a note of your new web address for their future reference.

Ideally, you should keep the old site active and pointing to the new site for as much as two years. That probably sounds like a long time, but users may have put links to you on their web site, and pages of that sort are remarkably poor in terms of update time, so when you move you may be getting old links pointing to you for months and months. In addition, people tend to automatically add pages they like to their browser's lists – the 'bookmarks' in Netscape Navigator and the 'favorites' in Microsoft Internet Explorer – and then either wait months between visits, or repeatedly forget to change the bookmark/favorites entry. To be fair, it takes a fair degree of computer knowledge to know how to edit a bookmark list, so people often leave old bookmarks as they stand because they aren't certain about how to revise them. Either way, it all lends itself to people using old, outdated links to get to your old site for a lengthy period of time, and if they try your old address and get nothing, they will assume you have gone out of business or closed down. This is equivalent to the real-world practice of moving a business to a more prestigious location.

Why not, also, invest in people? Maybe it is time for you to move up and learn some new skills… As you will have spent some time using a computer, it might be time to learn how they work at a deeper level and purchase new software to expand your mind. There are certainly a lot of things you could do yourself instead of giving the job to others, such as maintaining your own site, creating banners and graphics etc. You can also learn to operate high-end database software, or a financial program. There are books and university courses to help you in this task, so get to it.

Upgrading your computer, provided it is not a major revamping of the whole system, can also be an area where you can learn a thing or two. Adding some memory chips or a new hard disk drive, tuning up the beast – all this you can do. Remember that the more you do yourself, the less you will have to pay somebody to do it for you.

On the other hand, maybe it would prove worthwhile to get some help and employ somebody to take care of things while you go out and get some new contracts in. Expanding requires time and energy and, unfortunately, you still cannot zoom from place to place. So, while you wait for the Star Trek beam-me-up thingy to be out of the labs in Silicon Valley, balance your costs (including taxes) with your potential earnings and get someone in to help.

The final option is to invest your money into more promotion for your site. That does not really constitute an expansion as such – expanding your business adds tangible value to the business itself, making it worth more as a concern, whereas investing in more advertising and marketing is a way of spending money that does not leave behind any real, physical difference to your business. However, you may well find that your hit rate and profits are greatly increased by a good advertising campaign, which is why so many companies on and off the web spend so much money on it. So long as your campaign is a decent one, marketing and advertising should, generally, make back more for you than they cost you, although it's tricky to measure their effects. Still, it makes them an attractive and viable option when it comes to investing some profits back in your site.

SELLING YOUR SITE

Now you have your web site and thousands of visitors pass through daily. You're selling products or services, and may even be making some money after you've covered all your expenses. But you could struggle on for years and not make serious money. Longevity in the new economy is no indicator of success – when boo.com collapsed, it had been running for over a year, and Boxman traded for over three years before running out of money! Of course, you could go back for a second, third or even fourth round of financing to support your business, but that, in the long term, merely means someone else owns a larger chunk of you – no, your best solution in the quest to make those big bucks is to arrange things so as to make the most convincing case for your business as a valid proposition at *some time in the future* and then sell.

WHAT'S INVOLVED IN SELLING YOUR SITE

It really depends now on whether it is just a site that you're selling (which is, remember, just a set of files on a computer somewhere), or a whole company, with staff, customers, a brand identity and the promise of huge things to come.

If you're just selling a site, you'll need to be able to show the number of visitors it attracts, and ideally some information as to the type of people they are. You'll need to indicate whether the site stands alone, or whether a potential purchaser will need to engage someone to update it regularly. And then you need to set a price.

If, on the other hand, you now have a business behind your web site – editors, developers and designers who keep the site tip-top and up-to-date, customer service staff and fulfilment operatives who make sure that people can order and do receive whatever you're selling, and business development and management staff too – then selling your site is no different from selling a conventional company, save for the fact that the current climate indicates that a potential purchaser is more likely to pay for the possibility of success, rather than the actual track record a conventional business may need to prove.

Many Internet businesses are valued by the number of subscribers, or registered users, they have. We're still at the very beginning of understanding the new economy, and while the most sophisticated and forward-thinking analysts have offered various models for predicting the future profitability and value of Internet start-ups, they are as yet unproven. The most enduring rule-of-thumb valuation is $1,000 per registered user, so a web site with 10,000 users could well be worth $10,000,000 – that's ten million dollars!

HIT LOGS & USER RECORDS

You can see then that keeping an accurate record of the traffic on your site, along with a complete (and as in-depth as possible) database of your registered users is an absolutely vital first step towards selling your web site. Most web servers will keep logs of visits to your site, though the information isn't always terribly useful, and it's certainly unacceptable to make a business case based purely on server logs. (They can be useful, however, for supporting claims of click-thrus and for seeing from where people are referred when they visit your site – see Chapter 8: Promoting Your Web Site for more on this.) In order to add value to your site, you'll need to make sure that during the development process, measures are taken to record *at least* a username and password combination for individual users. There is no reason to try and charge people to register – that is not likely to be a major source of revenue, and you'll prevent the largest number of people from registering. You can also try and capture some demographic information – geographical location, age, sex, income, etc. – but again remember: the more information you ask for, the less inclined people will be to fill in all the questions just to access your site.

PROFITABILITY AND TURNOVER

If your business is very young, there is unlikely to be a correlation between

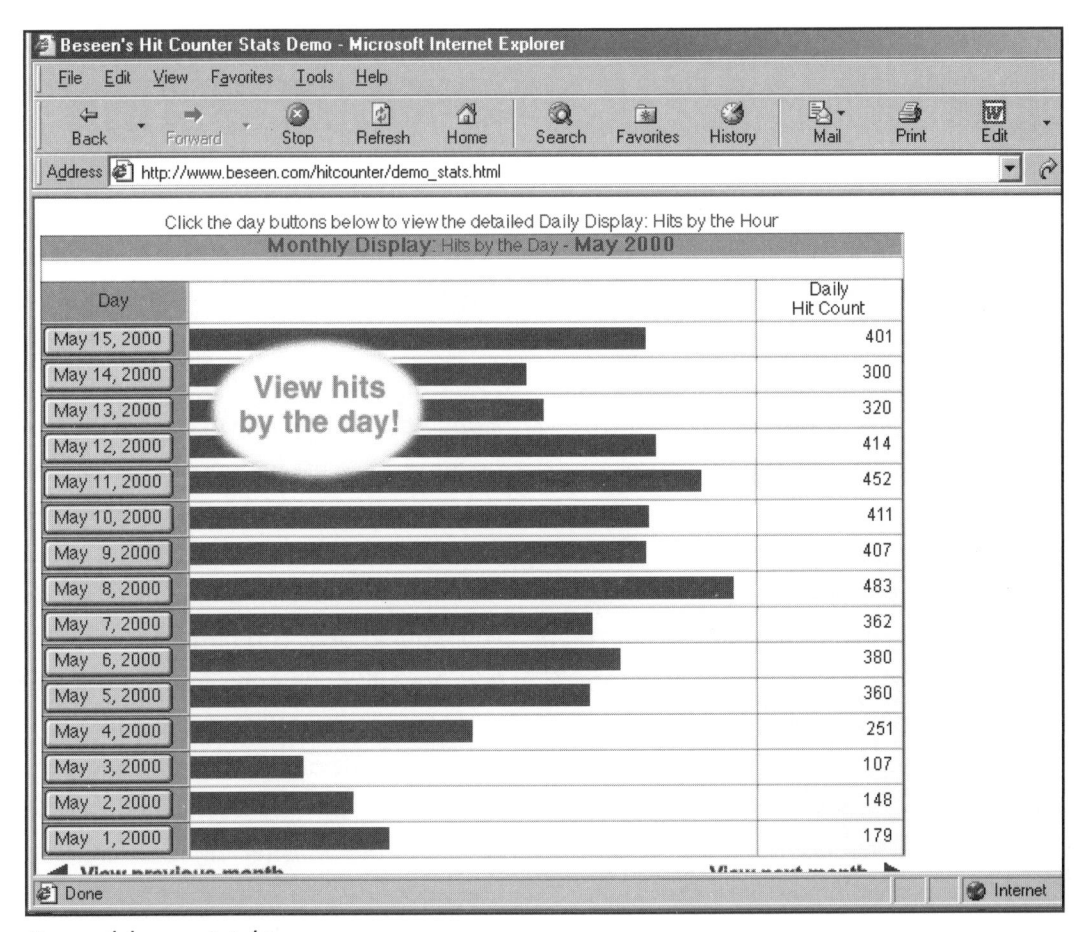

Know exactly how your site is doing.

turnover and profit. Only a tiny handful of Internet-based businesses outside of the porn sector have so far made any profit, even though some are actually turning over hundreds of thousands, and even millions, of pounds a year. The level of investment required to develop the business, to market it seriously, to pay staff and cover overheads normally takes all the money the company earns and more. But as we've said earlier, Internet-based companies are, in general, not valued on the amount of profit they make, but on the amount of profit that they *could* make, one day.

All the same, you need to be thinking of profitability from the very beginning. It is important that you keep good and accurate accounts, so early on, invest in a relationship with a good and reputable accountant – it will literally pay dividends later on. As you trade in the early days, you need to predict how your business will need to grow in order to first break even, and then to turn a profit. This book can't cover all the information you'll need to start up a business but any good bookstore ought to have many titles on the subject.

SELLING

The first thing you need to do in order to sell your company is to put a team together. You already have an accountant, and a management team, but you'll need a lawyer and quite possibly a banker. Try to get recommendations from people who've used the professionals you choose to work with you – they can make or break your deal and could cost you a large amount of money if they're not up to scratch. Check trade organisation memberships and ask to see a list of current clients. Ask also if they'd be prepared for you to contact a couple of the existing clients to talk about them and the service they've provided – if they refuse, think twice about engaging them.

It may also be necessary to engage a professional business broker. The Internet market is new and very few people have any specialisation in it, but the entire business market is so confusing these days that even your accountant and lawyer may feel the need for some specialist help.

The first task your team will face will be to price your business. Even though you're working with a professional team, you must keep in mind that the first prices you discuss may not be quite right – your lawyer and accountant will have a vested interest in not losing your account, and the broker may feel that all you want to hear is a huge figure. But if you price the company too high, it will take longer to sell, and then you're caught in a vicious circle – the longer it's on the market, the less inclined people will be to buy it. After all, if no-one else has bought it, there must be something wrong with it, surely?

If the broker you hire can't appraise the business, or the team can't agree on a price, you may consider going to an independent business appraiser – it may cost a couple of thousand pounds for the service but a prospective buyer may be more impressed to see you've done everything properly and professionally.

Along with a price, you need a comprehensive set of documents to tell buyers all about your business. Most people who'll be looking to buy your business will be professional money-men who expect a large amount of information handed to them on a plate – and don't forget, they won't be interested in any passionate argument about how much you believe in the business if they can't see the figures on the bottom line for themselves. Your accountant, banker, lawyer and broker will be able to advise you on all the documents you'll require, and will help you draw them up.

Once you and your team have completed your marketing package, you'll have a fairly good idea of the type of buyer you'll need. You'll know how much money they need in order to make your business work and your broker should be able to set up a process to target and qualify prospective buyers.

Your broker can arrange meetings with people who fit the right profile, but make sure he mentions upfront the amount of money you're expecting these people to need – there are a good number of timewasters out there who'll try to convince you that they can run your business "no money down" and pay you from the profits later. Don't go wasting your time.

It may also be worth mentioning at this point that businesses don't sell as quickly as houses. True, Internet businesses are very attractive to investors at the moment, and there is every chance that if you have a solid business proposition, a good offer will come along sooner rather than later, but don't panic if you've not sold in weeks – it could take months, or even a year.

Once you've got an interested prospect, you need to make sure that the negotiations proceed professionally and quickly – you are dealing with people who do this every day. Don't get bogged down in debate and don't allow your ego to blind you from to the fact that your underlying aim here is to sell. It's probably best to see the buyer as an ally – someone who's looking to make the deal as straightforward and beneficial to both parties as you are. Try to remain objective and business-like at all times.

If your prospect makes an offer you're prepared to accept, get it in writing as soon as possible – even the best buyer prospects can change their minds overnight so some security from the beginning gives you the opportunity to relax your search for another buyer, comfortable that you have actually found one. Ask them for a non-refundable deposit – that will shake out any waverers who are just saying 'Yes' to stop you selling to anyone else while they make up their mind. But remember, until you cash that cheque, anything can go wrong, so keep your eyes open at all times and be prepared for the whole thing to collapse around your ears and for you to have to get back onto the whole roundabout once again.

Of course, you may be lucky – a buyer may come to you, especially if you've managed to cultivate a good reputation and your PR and marketing have given you high visibility. Remember, though, a

Transfer or Surrender of Registration

Transfer of Domain Name Registration

Use this section if you wish to transfer the Domain Name registration to another organisation or person. Please read the following instructions carefully. We regret that we cannot process transfer requests using incomplete documents.

1. Both Declarations and the New Registrant Form below must be completed in full to transfer the Domain Name registration from the current Registrant (the Transferor) to another organisation or person (the Transferee). Please Note: A different person must sign on behalf of each party.

2. In addition, both Transferor and Transferee must submit signed, confirmatory letters on their official letterhead paper.

Transferor Declaration *(current Registrant)*
- I/we agree to Nominet UK's current Terms & Conditions found on the World Wide Web at www.nominet.org.uk/terms.html
- Please transfer the registration of the Domain Name overleaf to the new Registrant below.
- ▶ **I attach a signed confirmatory letter on our letterhead paper.**

Signature ....
Print Name ....
For & on behalf of ....
Position ....
Date date month year

Transferee Declaration *(proposed Registrant)*
- I/we agree to the transfer of the registration of the Domain Name overleaf to me/us on Nominet UK's current Terms & Conditions found on the World Wide Web at www.nominet.org.uk/terms.html
- I/we confirm that the details below are correct.
- ▶ **I attach a signed confirmatory letter on our letterhead paper.**

Signature ....
Print Name ....
For & on behalf of ....
Position ....
Date date month year

Details of new Registrant:
Registrant Name ....
Companies House registered number (if Ltd/Plc) ....

Keep your Certificate of Registration with Nominet in case you wish to sell your domain name.

buyer who comes to you needs to be checked just as thoroughly as one you find yourself – timewasters abound and it's your time they'll be wasting.

FLOATING ON THE STOCK EXCHANGE

If selling's not your thing, you can still make serious cash by floating your company on the stock exchange, while retaining (a certain degree of) ownership over the whole thing. Flotations are often the main aim of Internet-based companies, and initially, spectacular sums of money were raised by start-ups launching themselves onto the stock market. It's not taken long for that early furore to die down but even now, while it's less likely than before, a well presented floatation can make the founders very rich indeed.

When you decide to take your company to the market, you must enlist the help of an investment bank or a company of underwriters. You need to produce a prospectus, which is in part a marketing document and in part a declaration of the state of the business – your investment banker can help you with putting a prospectus together.

Many people use an IPO (Initial Purchase Offer) as, in the main, a marketing exercise – a lucrative IPO can garner great coverage and PR and offers a great deal towards brand building. Many Internet companies also use IPOs to fund expansion, or even to stave off foreclosure – remember, analysts still consider Internet companies that are not making a profit, if they can show that they're likely to make a profit in the future. The share-buying market out there is very similar, and will often invest in a company that is losing money and offers no reasonable dividends at the time of purchase, merely because of the promise of future success.

With Internet-based companies, the main stock exchanges are still a little wary, but NASDAQ in the USA happily takes around 75 per cent of all technology IPOs at the moment. Once again, talk to your investment banker.

To take your company through an IPO, you need to follow three steps. Firstly, you must analyse. This is often done by an underwriter, with the co-operation of you, your management team, you bankers and lawyers and your accountant. The underwriter will estimate your company's value, and determine the number of shares (and thus the percentage of your company) to offer.

A warning – while the valuation process is going on, your investment bankers will be carrying out a due diligence examination. This is an exhaustive process to ensure the accuracy and completeness of all the information about your company. Any slips-ups here could leave your flotation floundering before it even reaches the market.

Secondly you must register you company for IPO. If you're going to float on NASDAQ, you need to register with the SEC in the USA. (Need we say, talk to your investment banker?) This involves a lot of paperwork, and you will need to provide things such as a description of the business, management's discussion and analysis of the company's operations, information on the risks associated with the offering and a description of key members of the management team, including yourself.

Once you've registered, and you, your underwriter, and the SEC agree to issue stock until 90 days after the initial offering is complete, you are not allowed to try and raise interest in the stock – this is called the 'Quiet Period'. You are allowed to announce you will be offering stock, when, and at what price, but nothing more, save being able to distribute the draft copy of your prospectus to potential investors (known in the business as the 'Red Herring' due to the large red 'DRAFT' which must be printed on the cover.

Once the stock is priced and syndicated (distributed to a group of investment bankers, responsible for seeing it out into the investment community), your underwriter will exchange cash for stock, which will then be traded on the open market. Having received the proceeds from your flotation, you will need to file a report with the SEC stating how the money will be used. This process is called the 'Closing' and is the finalisation of an IPO.

At a later date, you may choose to release more stock onto the market to raise further funds, but remember, the more stock that's out there, the easier it is for someone to take a controlling interest in your company, and maybe even take it over. Stock holders are entitled to vote at company general meetings on resolutions which will affect how your company is run, so always try to keep a majority stake. If you're forced by circumstances to sell a major share of your company's stock, make sure that the deal includes a cast-iron guarantee that you will remain in some controlling position for a period of time, else you could find yourself out before your feet have touched the ground.

Again, we must reiterate, this book cannot possibly teach you how to float your company, but if this is a path you ultimately want to follow, take all the advice you can get and be prepared to invest money engaging professionals to help you. The distance between sitting in your bedroom developing a web site and an IPO is huge, and you can't be expected to traverse it alone. Taking a company through an IPO is, apart from anything else, an extremely expensive process and one that will consume a lot of time. The cowboy dream of thinking up a web site on Monday and being a millionaire by Friday has never really been feasible – on the one or two occasions when that did happen, the cash injection came in the form of private investment in the site on the part of extremely rich speculators, rather than as a stock market flotation.

Getting rich quick is always highly tempting, but equally highly unlikely. If you can track down a wealthy philanthropist or relative and persuade them that your site idea is unique, incredible and likely to be insanely profitable if you can just get it off the ground – and if you have a rock-solid business plan behind you to back it up, and a top-class domain name – then maybe, just maybe, you'll be able to get a huge pot of cash to develop your idea (but remember, spending it on yourself is fraud!). The chances of managing to pull it off are extremely remote at best. You might just be better off buying a lottery ticket and hoping that your 14 million to 1 shot will come off – it's more likely, quite frankly.

However, if you are realistic, and you want to run your site as a business because it is a business that interests you, and you're prepared to take the time to do it right and build up a customer base, then you'll start establishing yourself, with a little luck. Once that happens, perhaps you'll be in a position to look at selling up, or building on your success until you have the potential in place to go to IPO. Like all plausible routes to wealth, though, it involves skill, talent, almost all your time (free or otherwise) and, at the end of the day, also a lot of luck.

USING A WEB SITE TO ENHANCE YOUR CURRENT BUSINESS

There has been discussion of promotional web sites in the preceding pages, but so far we have concentrated mainly on sites that are supposed to actually generate money directly. In this section, we'll closely examine the whole basis of promotional web sites, giving a clearer picture of how to use a web site to enhance your current business. Promotional sites are swiftly becoming as indispensable to active companies as fax machines were in the early 90s – it is getting to the point in some sectors where any firm without a promotional web site is looked down upon as a second-rate operation.

Furthermore, many sourcing functions are now moving to the web throughout business and industry. Procurement executives are no longer thumbing through trade catalogues or searching the yellow pages, they're opening up Alta Vista and Yahoo! and doing web searches for the material they need. If your site isn't there to pass the message on that your products and services are available, you are missing out on one of the most critical aspects of your business-to-business communications.

As with any other commercial web site, visitors will expect reasonably fast site download times, professional-looking page design and an easily navigable site structure. Once that is dealt with, there are many different promotional functions that a web site of this kind can perform, and each one has certain expectations attached to it on the part of your visitors.

One of the most common elements of a promotional site is an overview of the business itself. This comes as a series of inter-connected pages showing images of your operation along with relevant information. Promotional corporate pictures like this normally include a flattering image of your business premises, both externally and internally (normally the reception area, meeting rooms, and/or other attractive areas). These could be linked to maps showing your location, and your postal address, written directions, a short overview of the company history, and so on. If you have a physical production facility, telemarketing suite or warehouse, then this could be included on a separate page, along with pertinent details of your facilities and what output you regularly achieve. Other common details include biographies, contact details and pictures of the managing director, key staff, and/or unusually photogenic front-line staff members.

A related element of a promotional site is a page or series of pages demonstrating exactly what you can do. This should include details and (where appropriate) images of past projects and successes, information about peak output levels and deliverables, and other items of corporate promotional material. Don't be shy in this section; treat it as you would your company brochure, and use it to make your site visitor understand exactly how good your firm is. Successful physical projects are always a good thing to include here because they provide you with an excellent opportunity to use images in the site, which makes the design more impressive. Always remember, of course, to keep individual pages short, so that they download quickly, but not so short that they are useless. An individual web page should correspond to one page of a brochure, not to one paragraph or to the entire document.

Equally important is to have a comprehensive product and pricing catalogue. Whatever it is that your business is offering, you need to make sure that it is fully listed and explained on your site. Don't automatically assume that a site visitor is going to fully understand your sector of the market. Extended explanations and instructions are unnecessary – you don't want to appear patronizing – but by the same token, allow sufficient description for the information to be usable. If you sell a range of goods, then include their technical specifications and full images (with the full-size image as a separate download, as described previously); if you provide a service, or make goods to customer orders, then give as much information about that as you can. Include representative samples to let people see the sort of work that you produce.

Less common – but extremely impressive to customers – is to provide order-tracking details on your web site for existing customers to make use of. The technical side of it is quite easy; provide a page for a customer to type their order number into, and then set up a script to cross-check that with a database of how things are progressing, and call the information up. Without an order number people won't be able to find the data, so there's little danger of casual browsers finding other people's details. You need to make sure that the progress database is kept current by updating the information on a daily basis, but that too can be largely automated.

A web page is also a perfect place to set out a number of important documents regarding your business dealings – the terms and conditions that you require from customers, and that you will accept from suppliers, any restrictions or legal issues that you might have, submission disclosure undertakings, confidentiality agreements, and so on. This is the sort of paperwork that many people will want to see before making a deal, and letting them have a look at it in advance saves all of you from a degree of wasted time and effort. Transparency in this regard is a valuable bonus in the modern marketplace.

As well as legal documentation, you should also have an area of your site dedicated to corporate communications and other bits and pieces of company information. Press releases should also be put up on the web, and might even have their own primary section if you issue a lot of them and anticipate significant press interest. Some companies like to provide a search engine to cross-reference through press release databases, to help visitors extract the information that they are after more readily. You can also include financial reports and investor information if you are a public company, issue statements and declarations, and in fact report just about any other piece of corporate information that you think beneficial for interested parties to be able to examine. At all times, though, remember to make sure that this sort of material is well organised and structured, so that visitors do not have to wade through a miscellany to get to the information they need.

Career opportunities are a staple of promotional web sites. There will always

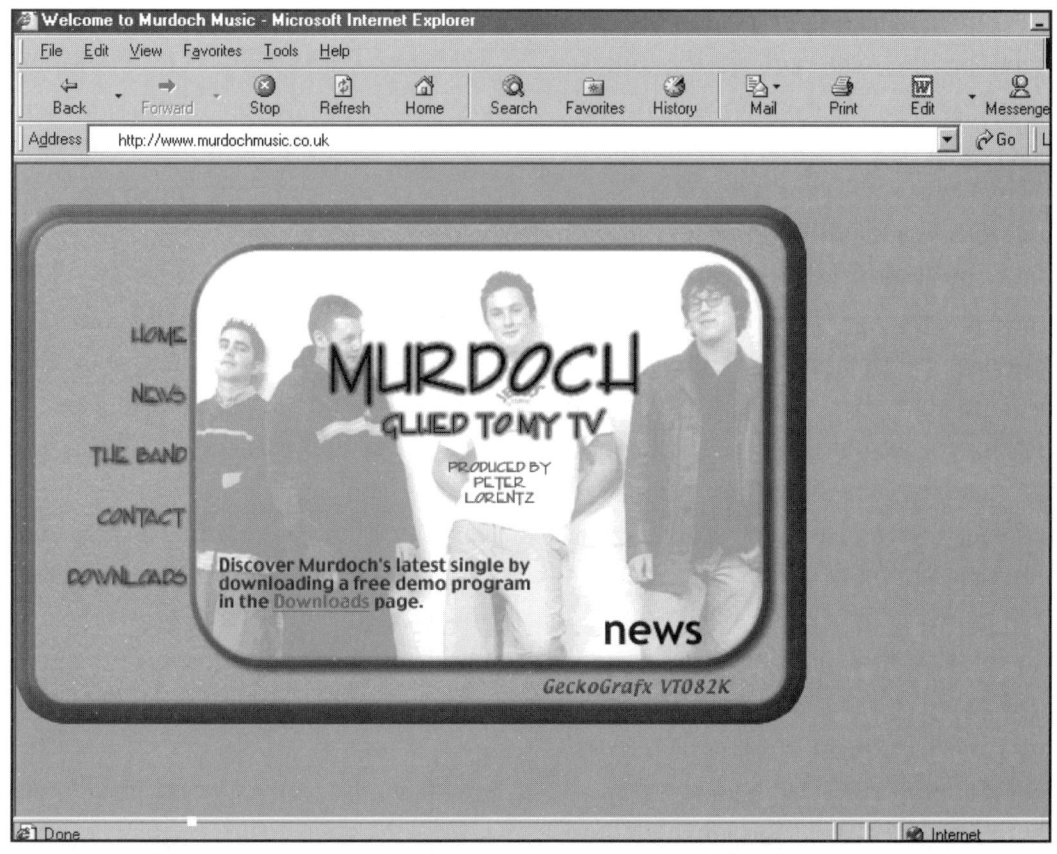

The web is a fantastic tool to promote such things as new bands. Haven't you got anything you want to advertise and share with millions of people?

---

be a certain subsection of site visitors who are interested in working for your company, and at the very least you should include details of whom to contact, what your recruitment policy is, and the email address that CVs should be forwarded to, along with the formats you will accept them in. More advanced recruitment sections will include a list of staff benefits and facilities, details of any pension and/or healthcare arrangements that you offer, and a full, searchable listing of all your current vacancies and the requirements that they have. This sort of section in your promotional site can significantly reduce your recruitment costs, if you treat surfing potential employees with the thought and respect that you treat surfing potential customers.

As a marketing aid to getting your site seen on the Net and having people come across your company through that, you can include one or more tribute areas on your site, on subjects relevant to your core business. This can be a particularly good way of getting new clients, particularly if the tribute area is extensive and well-designed. It will always be worth engaging a freelance writer to research and produce the content for you unless you already have professional writers working for you in-house. If you can make sure that the tribute subject is something that interests your core customer base, it doesn't even necessarily have to be directly relevant to your business. For example, a bespoke software programming house with a promotional site could include a tribute area reminiscing over and providing information on early arcade-based computer games, as these are a long-standing fondness and interest amongst the current generation of up-and-coming IT managers. If the tribute area is not of direct relevance to your business (as in the previous example) then links from the tribute site to the main promotional site should be large and obvious, but links from the promotional site to the tribute area should be small and tucked out of the way. You want surfers to hit the tribute site and go on to your corporate area. You do not particularly want clients to move away from your corporate area into your tribute site.

Other things that you can do mostly centre around enhancing the utility of your web site as a means of getting customers and potential customers to come back to it whether or not they are actually thinking of making use of your commercial services. Just by visiting your site they will be reminded of you and thus encouraged to engage you. Themed resources and/or entertainments that are pertinent to your business and fit in with your corporate profile are an excellent addition to any promotional site. Obviously, their nature is going to vary from company to company. A large multinational bank is not going to want to host an online interactive chess game, but it may well include up-to-the-moment currency converters, details of the current time and weather in every major international city, or a historical analysis of the copper trade in ancient China. A toy and game manufacturer, on the other hand, is going to feel exactly the opposite. Use a bit of imagination and ask yourself what you might be interested in or impressed by if you were a third party visiting your web site.

If you have a strong brand image for your company, you can also offer branded merchandising of all types or web-only special offers that physical customers could not make use of. This is only really appropriate if you expect the general public to visit your site, but if they are going to drop by, then it can be an excellent way of generating goodwill. Merchandising, in particular, can be an excellent opportunity to combine small-scale revenue generation with free marketing and the building of further goodwill. T-shirts are extremely popular items of merchandising with the younger parts of the population, and any strong brand will be able to carry off a tastefully understated item of clothing. For an older customer base, branded jackets, ties or lapel pins might prove popular. IT-related merchandise is also often successful, such as computer carry cases, mouse mats, floppy disks and so on. If you have a brand, it is foolish not to capitalise on it.

Everything else aside though, and irrespective of how many of the above elements you choose to employ in your particular site, you have to remember the three unbreakable rules of tribute sites.

Number one, do not try to extract cash from people using web business methods. No banners, no ad links, no membership fees, nothing. Branded merchandise is the only possible exception, and even then it should not be expensive.

Number two, do everything you can to make the site as user-friendly as possible. Do not demand registration (no matter how much you would like the customer data), do not provide misleading links, structure the site usefully, and provide a full suite of customer service facilities.

Number three, make sure the site is well written, both in terms of coding and, every bit as important, in terms of text. The Web relies on the written word, and if your writing is deficient in any way, your firm will also seem to be illiterate. Hire freelance writers if your company is not in the business of writing, and hire a Web design firm if your company is not in the business of Web design. You wouldn't try to produce your own TV advert if you were not in the business of filming ads, and a promotional site is similarly far too important to leave to amateurs.

Keep these issues in the front of your mind whenever you are considering the structure of your promotional site, and it will become an invaluable tool for your future business success.

GET PAID TO SURF

To some people, this sounds like a dream come true – the best thing since microwaved meals. Getting paid just for surfing... Sounds too good to be true! Well, it is true but is it any good? The answer to that depends on your attitude to small amounts of money and the length of time you are prepared to spend online, surfing shopping sites and reading adverts.

Some examples of the many Web sites offering reward schemes give a good idea of what to expect.

REWARD SCHEMES BY SITE

Alta Vista Rewards is a scheme, run by the well-known Alta Vista portal, that pays out points which may be redeemed once enough of them have been accumulated. Points can be collected in a number of different ways. Simply registering entitles the customer to up to 1,000 points. A maximum of 1,000 points per day can be earned by browsing the Alta Vista Shopping pages and the pages of participating vendors. Users can earn 25 points for visiting 'partner' stores and 5–25 points for clicking on designated links within those pages. In addition, every dollar spent on goods or services through Alta Vista's shopping pages earns 45 points. It can take up to seven days for points to be credited to your account. Points expire after two years if not redeemed. Points can be redeemed for goods listed in the reward catalogue. Goodies on offer include computer and electronic hardware, holidays, sporting goods and toys. Gift certificates are available but points cannot be swapped for cash, though they can be passed on to participating charities as a donation.

The reward catalogue starts at 2,500 points for a charitable donation. A Blockbuster voucher for $5 costs 5,000 points (giving a rough value of 0.1 cents per point). 20,000 buys a magazine subscription. Goods valued at more than 150,000 points are available but were unlisted at the time of writing.

Alta Vista's scheme is not yet available in the UK, however.

BEENZ.COM

Beenz.com is another scheme which pays in points or 'beenz'. Beenz may be exchanged for goods from the Beenz reward catalogue or participating vendors. The beenz.com site carries a list of participating advertisers. When visited, these sites will automatically credit beenz to your account – or, in some cases, members must click on a beenz icon to register their visit. Beenz.com also carries a list of vendors who will redeem beenz for goods.

Users are encouraged to get their friends to sign up, receiving beenz for each new member who signs up through them.

BeenzBack is a scheme whereby users are credited with beenz when making (paid for) purchases at participating sites. Logging-on to beenz.com takes members to a cookie-personalized page which shows beenz balance, last transaction and other account details.

Gift vouchers from the Beenz catalogue range from 3,500 beenz for a £10 voucher, to 31,200 beenz for a £100 voucher giving an approximate value of 0.3 pence per beenz.

ALLADVANTAGE.COM

AllAdvantage.com aims to deliver highly-targeted advertising to its users. To join the scheme users must first download the AllAdvantage viewbar and install it. The viewbar plugs into their browser and must be active during surfing to qualify for rewards.

When the user surfs into a participating site, an advert will be downloaded into the viewbar and displayed. The viewbar software reports to 'base' when the user is surfing and registers that user as eligible to receive rewards according to which reward scheme is chosen (selectable on a monthly basis).

Rewards can be gained in two ways: a sweepstake or the pay-per-minute Alternative Reward Scheme. The $50,000 sweepstake prize is distributed daily. Out of this, a $25,000 Grand prize goes to one lucky, randomly selected member, provided that they have qualified by surfing for at least three minutes that day with their viewbar on. Extra entries are awarded for each three minutes to a maximum of five entries or 15 minutes. The remaining 50 per cent is distributed to the next five members 'upstream' in the chain of referrals, ie, if Tom refers Dick, Dick refers Harry, Harry refers Bob, Bob refers Dave and Dave wins the sweepstake, Dave gets $25,000 and the others get $5,000 each.

If the Alternative Rewards Scheme is selected, the member is credited for any time that they spend surfing with the viewbar active, and a smaller amount for the surfing of any members they have referred too. Members get 2p for each hour of their own surfing, 0.06p for members one step downstream in their referral chain and 0.03p per hour for those two steps downstream.

There is a 12 hour per day maximum surfing time and cash cannot be claimed until at least £18 is accrued.

MONEYFORMAIL.COM

MoneyForMail.com claims to be the first company on the Net to offer to pay its members cash for reading email. In common with other email schemes, this is a misnomer, since it is not reading the email that qualifies members for payment but following an embedded hyperlink to the advertiser's site where the advert actually is.

After filling out a detailed user profile, members can opt for one of two levels of membership: Standard membership offers 20 to 50 cents per mail 'read'. Advanced membership allows the user to append an authenticated credit-rating to their profile. Advanced users are prioritized for ad distribution and get paid 25 cents to $2.50 per mail. Payouts are monthly, by cheque, beginning as soon as the minimum $10 is accumulated.

INBOXDOLLARS.COM

InboxDollars.com is an email reward scheme that pays out cold, hard cash. Members can sign up direct at the site or via a URL supplied by a referrer. After completing a form detailing their user profile and interests, users can select categories of goods and services in which they are interested and wish to receive email advertisements for. These emails should, as a result, be directly related to things that the member is quite likely to spend money on. When the emails are received, the reader must click on an embedded link to the advertiser's web site in order to read (or at least take a cursory glance at) the advert. Users are credited with 5 cents for every email read and 2 cents for each email acknowledged by any 'downstream' referrals.

InboxDollars pays by cheque, monthly.

ALLCOMMUNITY.COM

The (public-facing) mission-statement of

this company is to 'Redistribute the Internet economy'. AllCommunity describes itself as a community of on-line surfers, pooling consumer strength. This bulk buying power is used to win members discounts and special deals like cashback. When purchases are made from AllCommunity itself, up to half the profits are redistributed to other members. They also act as an ISP, charging $19.95 per month.

In addition, members have access to four different types of reward scheme. Revenue Scheme 1 is an email scheme. Members selecting this package are paid 3 cents per email link they follow, and 1 cent for each email link followed by up to three layers of downstream referrals.

Revenue Scheme 2 requires members to buy a dialup account from AllCommunity at $19.95 per month. Members are paid 50 cents per month for every direct or indirect referral who uses their AllCommunity dialup account. This scheme does not pay out for your own surf time, only your referrals.

Revenue Scheme 3 pays you to surf with their ad-bar active on your screen. They pay 50 cents per hour for your own surfing, 10 cents an hour for direct referrals and 5 cents per hour for indirect referrals. There is a limit of 40 hours per month for each member.

Revenue Scheme 4 pays members to shop on participating sites. When purchases are made from AllCommunity shops, points are awarded which may be redeemed for cash at the end of the month at a rate based on AllCommunity's profits.

HOW THEY PAY

Internet and email reward schemes work on broadly the same principle. The operating company is a combination of a market research and internet marketing company. The active principle is that advertising is more cost-effective when carefully targeted at the people who are statistically most likely to buy your product. This increased value makes advertisers willing to pay more per customer exposed to the advert than 'broadcast' shotgun-style campaigns because it is still cheaper than trying to show the advertising to everyone.

Achieving this is difficult for the advertisers themselves, as intensive market research is costly and time-consuming and beyond the in-house resources of most vendors. It is far more practical to retain a third party to find your target audience. Traditional market research relies upon either cold-calling, street canvassing or embedding questionnaires in the applications for prize draws. Reward schemes are an ingenious way of getting the buying public to come to you and fill out their own profile for you. The incentive – cash – comes from a proportion of the advertisers' fee being trickled down to the scheme members.

Adverts are accepted by the marketeers and forwarded only to those who have previously expressed an interest. The advertisers are buying a service, not a list of names and addresses. Indeed, all sites promise that the members' details will never be passed to third parties. The delivery of adverts can be by emails (containing links to the advert pages which must be followed) or as banner ads that appear in a proprietary viewbar on the desktop. Different ads will be downloaded to different members' viewbars from any given participating site dependent on the users' profile. The viewbar will upload data such as ads viewed or time online to the reward site to be credited to the member's account.

Such is the apparent success of this, that, given that some schemes pay 5 cents per email viewed, it stands to reason that each advertiser is paying more than this per email sent, which could add up to a huge amount. This also means that the adverts will probably be of a higher quality than your average carpet-bombing spam.

A common feature of all schemes is that there are incentives to get members to actively recruit others. The more referrals, the greater a recruiter's potential income, as members are credited small amounts whenever their referrals earn credits themselves. The bonus to the reward scheme is that it cuts their own advertising overheads as many hopeful members spend hours of unpaid time 'referring' new members for them.

PAYING OUT

Accumulating credits or cash is all well and good as long as you can get your hands on some goodies at the end of the day. Schemes vary in the methods by which rewards of points and cash are accrued but all pay out in one of two similar ways. Points schemes work like the bonus schemes run by many credit card companies or supermarket loyalty cards. Accumulated points can be exchanged for a limited range of goods or services listed in the scheme's reward catalogue. Points can never be exchanged for cash. This is to prevent members from divining a set cash value for their points which would enable them to make meaningful guesses about the prices of the goods on offer. The stated price is a retail price and much less than the scheme paid for it. For example, points exchanged for a £100 camera appear to be worth £100. However, if the cameras are bulk-ordered from the catalogue at a unit price of £50 the real value of the points is correspondingly less. This is the purpose of points and catalogues as opposed to cash. Members who are accruing cash credits which may be spent anywhere must genuinely save £100 before they can get the putative camera. This costs the scheme £100 in cash payouts where a rival points-based scheme would have parted only with a £50 camera. Even gift vouchers (tied to participating stores) cost the scheme less than their face value.

Cash schemes pay out by cheque (some contriving to transfer money by email) but all have a minimum sum ranging from $10 to $100 which must be accumulated before anything can be claimed.

Currently, there are a great many competing reward schemes, all fighting for advertisers' money. Members who sign up for struggling or johnny-come-lately schemes may well find that they must surf for many many hours before coming across participant sites which can download 'scoring' ads to their advertising bar. In the UK, where, firstly, there are likely to be fewer participant vendors and, secondly, most people still get charged for local phonecalls, the income generated will do little more than offset their phonebill, even if they make hunting down Beenz, or whatever, a full-time pursuit. On analysis, the only way to make more than your phonebill is to spend considerable time persuading others to join up. This saves the schemes a great deal of money.

THE DOMAIN NAME GAME

A good domain name is vital to any Internet start-up company. Existing firms expanding onto the Net will usually want to use their own name or a variation of it. When selecting a new domain name it is crucially important to choose well. A name must be memorable and appropriate to the nature of the business. URLs will need to be advertised somehow outside the World Wide Web. A URL that neither trips off the tongue nor slips easily into memory will rarely get typed into a browser. For similar reasons it should, ideally, be short to limit the scope for mistyping.

HOT NAMES AND INSIDE INFORMATION

But what if everyone already knows the name of your business? If so, potential customers looking for your site may just try typing: COMPANYNAME.com into their browser or favourite search engine, expecting to be led straight to your site. Indeed, this often works. Except, that is, when some enterprising person has registered your name already.

This sort of thing was rife in the early frontier-days of the Internet. Those in-the-know early on in the game registered just about every household name they could think of. At the time, domain names were not effectively protected under law from trademark infringement. Large corporations found themselves having to pay out hundreds of thousands (and rumoured millions) of dollars to private individuals who had speculatively registered their names. Recently, domain speculators tried to beat the Disney Corporation to the domain name '102dalmations', losing out only because they could not spell 'dalmatians'!

By now, all the major monikers have been accounted for but there is still great potential for making money by pre-emptively registering desirable domain names. The secret is to anticipate what is likely to be a hot property next week, month or, indeed, next year. Examples might be: small companies about to make the big-time, up-and-coming pop-bands or foreign .coms expanding into the UK and needing a .co.uk address.

Also profitable are common mistakes, misspellings or abbreviations of big names. Many companies like to register a collection of similar-sounding URLs to anticipate people's most likely guesses as to what their address might be. Failure to do this for some organizations can lead to embarrassment. An American Presidential candidate recently used HISNAME.org as his official campaign site. A wily rival group, however, bagged HISNAME.*com* and used the site to lampoon the unhappy Republican. Spelling errors and other oversights can be worth money!

There are a multitude of methods that domain name speculators might use to decide on what names to register, from poring minutely over the records at Companies House to throwing darts at the alphabet. Whatever the strategy used, the process is likely to be similar to choosing lottery numbers.

Here are the rules:
- Only alphanumeric characters (eg, a, b, c, 1, 2, 3) and hyphens (-) can be used to create a domain name.
- Domain names are not case sensitive.
- Domain names must not contain spaces. These are usually replaced by hyphens.
- The domain name must begin and end with an alphanumeric character.
- Global domain names (eg, .com, .net, .org) must be no longer that 26 characters, including the suffix (4 characters).
- UK domain names (eg, .co.uk, .org.uk, .plc.uk, .ltd.uk) must be no longer than 63 characters, excluding the suffix.

In general, domain names are more valuable if they are short and punchy, avoiding anything prone to common errors of spelling – unless that is what you want. A quick survey of some auction site listings will give you a good idea of what people are betting on. Everyone's dream is to come upon some existing yet unexploited brand-name and beat a huge corporation to registration by scant seconds then milk them for millions... well, we can all dream. The best bet, rather than beating your brains out looking for a sure thing, is to keep your ear to the ground, study trends and look to the future. One day, 'Ticket-to-the-moon.com' might be in demand by British Airways. New technologies, new fashions – especially underground trends – and buzzwords from leisure pursuits, from abseiling to yachting.

Look for the emergence of new jargon words in the news and media. Words like 'spin-doctor', for instance, that we did not hear ten years ago. If, of course, you simply overhear a pair of city gents discussing a new start-up, then it is between you and your scruples as to what you do with the scoop.

People's names are fair game. Anyone, after all, could be called Tony Blair and have a dot com. Personal names cannot be trademarked, although professional or stage names may come with lawyers attached. Most domain names are common words, or combinations thereof, but many noted sites have used made-up words, like the ill-fated Kibu.com. Acronyms are also well worth looking at, though most of the shorter combinations are being snapped up apace.

One more field to explore is that of regular events such as sporting fixtures. These can represent some narrow windows of opportunity. Euro2000.com would clearly be worthless now as a football site but what about Euro2004, or Euro 2016? Think ahead.

When a promising name, or a selection thereof, has been chosen, the next step is to make sure that no one has beaten you to it. The early bird catches the worm every time.

CHECKING AVAILABILITY

The apparatus for the administration and allocation of domain names has been cobbled together ad hoc as demand for territory on the burgeoning World Wide Web has grown exponentially. The first authority in the early days of the proto-web was the Internet Assigned Numbers Authority (IANA). In 1984 the modern Domain Name System appeared, introducing the 'top-level' domains (three-letter suffixes): .com, .org, .net and .edu. In 1992 a quasi-governmental body called InterNIC was formed to administer the DNS and the non-profit corporation ICANN was created to foster competition between third parties offering to process applications for domains and contribute to the DNS database. This is the Shared Registration System in operation today.

Accredited domain registrars, usually for a fee, act as intermediaries between public and the relevant authority (ie, InterNIC for .com names, Nominet for .co.uk), handling all necessary research and bureaucracy. Whoever registers your domain, they will ultimately be dealing with InterNIC or the government-approved administrative authority of a country. Administrative authorities charge a registration fee. In the case of InterNIC this is $30 per year for a minimum of two years. Nominet charges £94 per two years. Nominet discounts this fee to its members (accredited registrars) by almost 95 per cent. This discount is rarely passed on to the consumer in its entirety by registrars and accounts for their profit-margin and the wide variety of prices. In effect the first £5 or so of your registration fee is Nominet charges. There is a list of Nominet members at http://www.nic.uk/members/members.html

There are already in the region of 19 million domain names registered and up to 40,000 new ones registered every day. All great minds think alike (and fools seldom differ) so if you think that a particular domain name is pretty cool, then chances are that one of the other 6 billion people knocking about the planet will too. Finding out if a particular name is taken already is simplicity itself. There are search forms specifically for this purpose on the pages of most, if not all, search engines and directories. Such searches are usually free – do not bother with any that ask for money for just a search. Simply type the domain name you have in mind and ensure that the correct top-level domain (eg, .co.uk or .com) is selected and the search will return an answer in seconds. Some search only for the specified top-level domain or domain type. Others will tell you if the name is in use with any of the 192 country-specific top-levels. This last type of search may not be instantaneous or free. The site Checkdomain.com offers a quick and easy search facility.

FINDING SOMEONE TO REGISTER WITH – ACCREDITED DOMAIN REGISTRARS

There are a multitude of Internet companies just queuing up to register your domain name. A quick trawl through a selection of them will show almost as many differing price structures and packages. Some offer a bare-bones deal whereby they process your application for a one-off fee and notify you when your annual admin fees to InterNIC (or equivalent) fall due, usually two years after your initial registration. Others offer to either host your web site on their server or at least to forward surfers and your email to your existing account (typically your domestic account). Some even offer web-mastering services. Following are some examples of such companies.

NETWORK SOLUTIONS (NETWORKSOLUTION.COM)

The original registrar, Network Solutions was very close to the process that created the DNS in the first place. The services offered on their web site are divided between those aimed at small-scale and domestic users under the umbrella of ImageCafe and those aimed at larger concerns, under the banner of idNames.

ImageCafe offers generic .com/org/net domains for $9.95 a month, including hosting. This comes to $238.80 over the two-year minimum purchase period and includes hosting. Of this amount, $60 will be InterNIC fees. By contrast, idNames offers generic domains for only $68 and country-specific domains

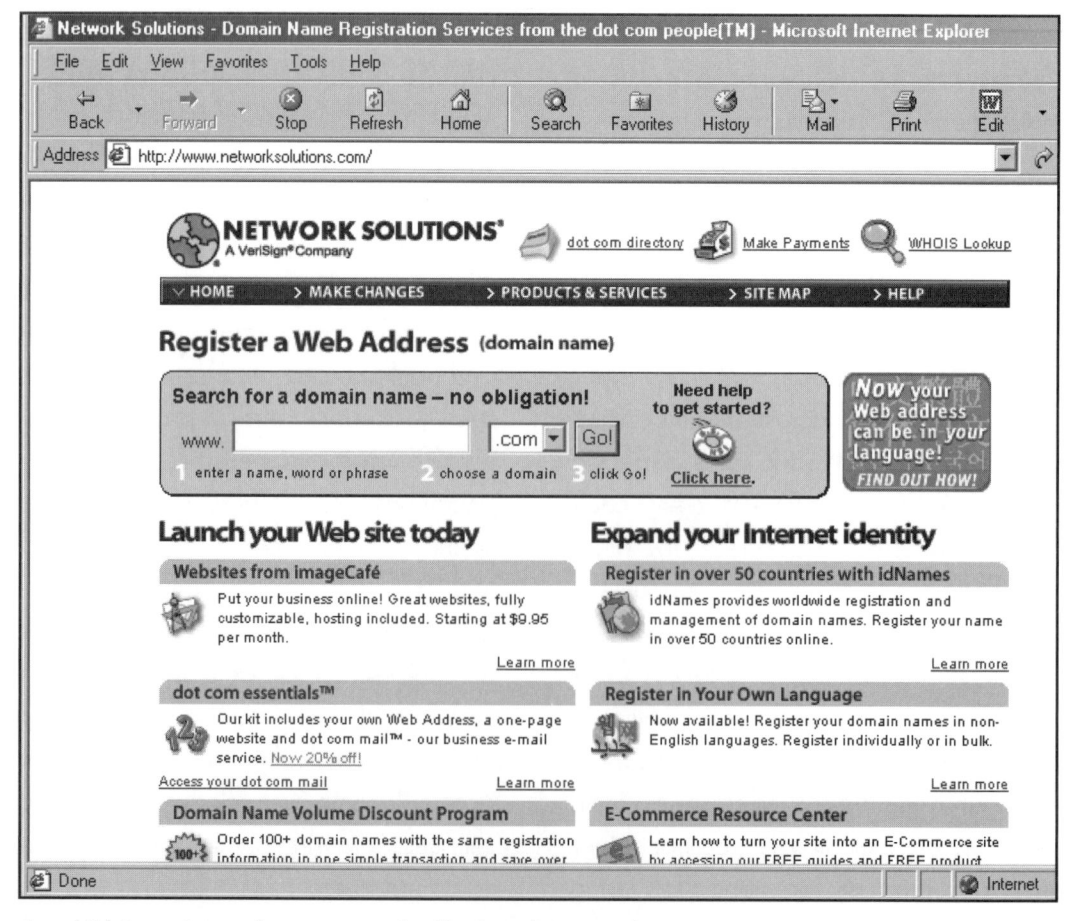

Network Solutions are just one of many companies who will register a domain name for you.

for $199. Network Solutions explain that country-specific domains are more costly to register since the prices, registration procedures and legal requirements vary from country to country and may be complex. Also, not being Nominet members means that it would cost them roughly $110 to register a .co.uk domain unlike a UK-based registrar.

NS also offer the facility to register anonymously, such that your name does not appear as owner on the WhoIs database at $250 for generics and $450 for others.

Network Solutions are a big, grown-up company who like to deal with big, grown-up clients. The solidity of their reputation is what attracts clients and allows them to charge fees that would deter more casual clients. After all, $450 is pocket change to a multinational.

R&D MILLENNIUM COMPUTERS (RD2000.CO.UK)

R&D are a UK-based company and Nominet member. They offer UK domains for £17.63 for two years. Generics are more, at £41.63 (remember the $30/year InterNIC fee?), and the new top-levels like .uk.co come in at £64.63.

Also available is EVAP, a service whereby any email name can be created @domainname.co.uk, and web-forwarding will divert emails to those addresses to your existing account. EVAP costs £29.38.

WHARF.UK.NET

This company is based in Canary Wharf and is a Nominet member. Basic domain name registration is £24.95 for a .co.uk and £34.95 for a .com, with web hosting starting at £99.

The basic package includes two year's Nominet registration, masked URL forwarding (so your Freeserve hobby-site can masquerade as a multinational), email forwarding and monthly search engine submissions so your page will never drop off the map.

HOW MUCH CAN YOU EXPECT TO PAY?

As can be seen above, prices vary considerably, along with the services in the package on offer. The cost-price of domain names for the minimum of two years is $30 if registered with InterNIC and around £5 if registered with Nominet through a Nominet member. Offers of 'Free!' domain names will almost certainly require the customer to buy hosting services, into the price of which the registration fee will be built back. A few companies offer very cheap registration, at practically cost price, as a loss-leader to attract customers to their web-hosting services and email forwarding.

The price differential has led some UK consumers to believe that .com domains are more desirable than .co.uk ones. This is only the case if your business is truly international in its scope and the reverse is true if your small-town window-cleaning business doesn't want to waste time turning down enquiries from Albuquerque. The difference is due solely to the fee policies of the responsible authorities. Currently, newly introduced domain extensions are priced at a premium – in some cases 50 per cent more than a .com – due to their novelty and desirability.

At the bottom line, a Nominet registration cannot cost less than £5 for two years, and InterNIC $60, whether paid in a lump or over two years. Neither Nominet nor InterNIC will defer fees. One has to ask, though: if a registrar is charging rock-bottom prices, how do they fund any technical support that you might need?

LEGAL ISSUES

In theory, there should be no legal problems at all relating to domain name ownership – so long as the words used are generic and cannot have been trademarked. For example Jurassic.com and Park.org would be fine but JurassicPark.co.uk (if not already in use) would have half the lawyers in Hollywood penning you sharp notes.

In cases of dispute over the ownership of a domain name, the registering authority, Nominet, is supposed to resolve the argument and in theory has the last word. Failure to accept their judgement gets you thrown to the lions – sorry, to the lawyers.

As a rule, in this increasingly litigious society, people, and corporations in particular, are very ready to go to court even when the ostensibly responsible authority has ruled against them. If, however, you aim to sell a name on and your asking price is less than their putative legal fees then you may be onto a winner anyway.

SELLING BY AUCTION

As previously suggested, a domain name does not need to be used as a web site URL in order to make money for you. For as long as your Nominet or InterNIC fees are paid up, the name is yours – barring *force majeure*. If anyone else wants the name for their domain, they will have to make you an offer.

Currently, the most common way to do

this is by auction and a number of sites have sprung up which virtually automate the whole process, from registering the domain to handling bids and payments. Some outfits prefer that you register your site through them or even insist that they host it (for at least two years). In these cases they might not be taking any commission on auction sales. Others make their profits purely from auction commissions.

Once you have registered your domain name you can put it up for auction on one of many sites simply by completing a form including the URL, the reserve price and a closing date for auction and your contact details. The reserve price is shown next to the name on the list page. This is updated as bids come in. Bidding is simply a matter of clicking a 'bid' button or link next to the name and entering a figure. When the closing date is reached, provided that your specified reserve price has been met or exceeded, the domain name goes to the highest bidder, with the auction company handling the transaction. The buyer is responsible for paying re-registration fees to Nominet or whoever and, dependent on their ISP, may incur charges for transfer of the domain name to a different server.

While most domain names sell on for little more than the original registration fee, a few gems go for lots, lots more. Recent examples are:

   hospitality.com – $230,000
   loans.com – $3,000,000
   cinema.com – $700,000
   phonecalls.com – $120,000
   act.com – $500,000
   perfect.com – $94,000
   happybirthday.com – $55,000
   bbc.com – £200,000 (purchased from its owners: the Boston Business Corporation)

SOME AUCTION SITES
http://www.auction2.net

This one is part of the UK2.net group of sites. All sorts of stuff is auctioned from this site. Users may only put up for auction domain names that are hosted by UK2.net. The good news is that UK2 charge only pennies per month (for two years). Inclusive of Nominet fees, this comes out at 38p a month with web-forwarding thrown in (the UK2.net will be appended to your URL in their browser window).

Auction2 manages to provide these amazingly low prices because it doesn't take any commission from auction sales, making their profits from similarly cheap hosting services. Anyway, it works for you too, which is the main thing.

http://www.sellmydomain.co.uk

There are three lists of names for auction on this site, divided between different types of top-level domain. Auctioneers can put their inventions up for either of two different types of auction, 'standard' or 'quick'. Standard auctions typically run for about three months and proceed at a sedate pace for those who really think they have a hot property and want to make sure that they get the very best price. Quick auctions are for sellers asking a lower reserve price and looking for a swift turnover, typically within the week. Commission is taken on sales as follows: up to £2,000: 20 per cent; between £2,000–£1,000: 15 per cent; over £10,000: 10 per cent.

There is a domain name valuation service costing £35 a throw, whereby your name is examined by experts who will base their estimates on their expert opinion. This is more useful to a company looking to sell on its own domain name rather than someone speculatively registering several.

http://www.domains-4-sale.com

This site claims to offer a free service to sellers of domain names. Of course, the domain must be registered beforehand, via Domains-4-Sale or not. The site appears to subsist on advertising, though this remains unobtrusive. In operation, it works much as do other sites.

http://www.domainbook.com

This US site has a catalogue which is sortable alphabetically by name, category, top-level and even length. There is a one-off posting fee of $19.95 per domain. Domainbook takes no commission. For $24.95 you can include a sales-pitch explaining the value of the name to those who don't yet see it and offering any associated services like webmastering. There are large discounts for bulk postings, starting at 50 per cent for ten and rising to 90 per cent for 100.

http://www.afternic.com

Another US site, Afternic is a well-featured and useful site with a keyword-searchable catalogue and useful automated proxy-bidding system which means that bidders can instruct it to up their bid by the minimum increment whenever they are outbid – up to a set limit. It is one of the longest-standing and best-known sites for domain auctioning, and is well worth consideration as a first port of call.

TRADITIONAL ADVERTISING

If you want a web site to make money,

people have to know about it. Fundamentally this means that, by hook or by crook, you have to get the name in front of people's eyes or trickle it into their ears. There are old and established methods of doing this, mostly involving paying huge sums of money to have a man go on radio or TV and shout it at people enthusiastically every 20 minutes, TV having the advantage that viewers get to read it at the same time.

Early on, advertisers thought that curiosity would encourage people to surf onto the site to see what it was about even if the brand adverts gave no clue. This proved not to be the case, as spectacularly demonstrated by a series of orangey-coloured TV and hoarding adverts for a vanished startup whose name has since slipped from the publicists' memory. National advertising campaigns are the stuff of big business and beyond the means of most. Local cable, radio channels or papers are cheaper but any meaningful campaign will still cost and probably require the services of a marketing company. A small boxed ad in a local paper costs upwards of £20 per issue and may have to run for weeks before it makes any impression on the readers. If funds are available, online marketing companies can undertake targeted mailing campaigns and banner advertising.

If you are a very small business or on a shoestring budget, there are a number of things you can do. Any office stationery or business cards (to be tossed around like confetti) can be modified to include your shiny new URL. In these cases it is considered acceptable to leave out the 'http://' and 'www' in the name of aesthetics. In fact anything that you own that is remotely customer-facing, including your car, could be plastered with your domain name. Tastefully, of course.

The next step up is bulk snail mailings. To avoid wasting your time and losing your ad in the background noise of junk mail, it is better to purchase, from a market research company, a list of people who have stated an interest in receiving advertising on specific topics. The same can be done by email but then it is doubly important to use an 'opt-in' list of willing recipients, because sending unsolicited advertising emails can get you in trouble with your ISP, and will do little more than alienate your audience. The same can be said of advertising in inappropriate newsgroups on Usenet. Spam advertising is very cheap and very nasty and only cheap, nasty outfits do it.

Another common method of drawing more hits to your site is banner advertising. There are some free services called banner exchange programs. Your advert is shown on other people's sites. In exchange, you must display on your front page a banner which downloads a selection of other people's adverts from the program's server. The downside is that you have no control over what is advertised from your front page. It could be one of your competitors, or something you find distasteful. Another type of banner advertising, which must be paid for, inserts your banner on a number of sites, chosen for their suitability.

If networking, in the personal sense, is your strong suit, then you could arrange a small-scale banner exchange amongst like-minded operators.

Failing any of the above, the least that you must do is to make sure that you submit your URL to as many search engines and web directories as is humanly possible. There are services you can pay to submit your URL and description to a whole swathe of directories. If you are on a zero budget, then spend a couple of evenings doing it yourself. The process is relatively easy, with most search pages having a link from their front page to their URL submission form.

THE NEW DOMAIN EXTENSIONS

The three-letter-suffixes or top-level domains most familiar to us are: .com, .co.uk, .org and a sprinkling of others. The full list (excluding non-UK country specifics) is:

GENERIC OR WORLD DOMAINS

com   Commercial businesses
org   Non-commercial organizations such as charities
net   Network providers (and other general sites)
edu   Educational establishments

UK SPECIFIC DOMAINS

co.uk   Commercial businesses within the UK
org.uk Non-commercial organisations within the UK, eg, British charities
ltd.uk Limited companies within the UK
plc.uk Public limited companies within the UK
ac.uk   Academic organisations within the UK
gov.uk All UK government departments/agencies (except defence)
mod.uk All Ministry of Defence establishments within the UK

lea.uk   All schools within the UK
nhs.uk   National Health Service organisations within the UK
net.uk   Network providers within the UK

OTHER UK DOMAINS

Newly created top-level domains include .tv which is intended for the emergent web-TV industry. People will expect such sites to be heavy on video-streaming content at high bandwidth.

Applicants may, in some cases, be required to show that they have the right to a top-level of a given category. Obviously .gov.uk and .mod.uk domains are not available to the public at all.

The introduction of new domain categories opens up the possibility of duplicating existing names that are registered under .com or .co.uk. Companies who already own their chosen domain, in both .com and local variants, may even now be rushing to register again as, for example, a .uk.co. Perhaps for this reason, the new domain names are priced considerably higher by the registrars, though there is nothing to suggest that Nominet fees are any higher.

Everything considered, though, the only domains worth worrying about for those in the UK at the time of writing are the .co.uk and .com domains. All other countries have their own suffixes.

YOUR FINANCES MADE EASY – BANKING ON THE NET

Banking has changed over the last few years. The main goal of all banks is getting the largest possible bottom Line. With the increase of computerized automation in this essentially mathematical business, many bankers are realizing that they can dispense with all those costly personnel and prime high-street corner locations. Low-profit or loss-making branches are being closed down. Inconvenienced customers who can afford it are turning to the internet.

There are a number of different ways in which money can be managed over the Internet, provided by both diversifying high-street banks and new, Internet-only startups.

INTERNET-ONLY ECASH BANKS

Of course, it's all very well having legions of goods for sale at the click of your mouse on the Internet but you still have to pay for it somehow. For the cautious, there is still the good old cheque or postal order via snail mail. For the more confident, there are credit cards, though giving out their number over the electronic ether still gives some people an attack of the nerves, even now that secure credit card servers are making transactions as safe as handing your card over in a restaurant.

Years ago, to address this issue, a number of companies like DigiCash.com came up with a method of securely exchanging credit between buyers and sellers. The name for these schemes was 'electronic cash'. In general, eBankers were supposed to pay for the technology (software) to process ecash transactions, while buyers downloaded free customer-facing client software. Anyone with the client software could both send and receive ecash.

Digicash's system used notional 'coins' or 'ecash'(tm) of differing denominations. Each coin was a packet of code which was to be digitally signed by the issuing ebank. This made each coin unique so that any attempt to directly copy coins would be recognized. It also meant that, if your virtual cash got deleted or your hard drive had a funny turn, the coins could be replaced like travellers' cheques (provided you had recorded the serial numbers in a safe place).

DigiCash.com was not a bank and only licensed the software to issuing ebanks. Merchants needed to know no more about customers than their host name – not even that if an anonymous remailer was used.

Other systems allowed you to buy credits on their servers and would then let subscribing companies accept payment in credits, transferring over the equivalent cash value – virtual debit cards for people who didn't have cards of any sort.

Initially the uptake looked promising, with such major players as Deutsche Bank and Nomura preparing to issue eMarks and eYen. Unfortunately, the system only really appealed to those too shy to buy 'adult' goods and services without cosy anonymity. When credit card transactions were made more secure, the established infrastructure of the card companies froze out this fledgling niche. Ebanking never really got out of beta testing.

REAL BANKS ON THE INTERNET

Most banks and building societies now offer access to your account(s) via the Internet. Naturally, to deposit cheques, withdraw cash or have a meeting with a bank manager, you must still find an open branch. Anything else, like checking your balance, interaccount transfers, paying into creditors' accounts, and bill payments can be done from wherever you can find Internet access, anywhere in the world (provided that you have the payees' bank details available). Bank web sites will also have links to pages dedicated to their other services like insurance and loans.

Signing up for an Internet portal to your bank account is straightforward but actually takes a few days. This is because your membership and password codes must be sent out to you by terrestrial mail. These codes give access to your money, so they must be kept secure. Some sign-up pages include stern warnings not to let your keyboard be overseen by CCTV cameras and to be wary of accessing your account from LANS or iCafes where you are not intimately familiar with their security. In addition to this, some forms request up to three personally memorable details in order that you can prove your identity if challenged. Many but by no means all require that your browser accepts cookies (for your 'convenience'). Most prefer that you use late versions of either Internet Explorer or Netscape Navigator/Communicator for compatibility and security reasons. None seem to mention other browsers, like Opera or iCab.

Transactions are managed through a simple form – simplicity helping to avoid confusion. For example, for credit transfers, the relevant accounts eg, current and savings, are selected from drop-down menus and the chosen amount entered in a box. All that remains is to click on a 'transfer' link and the transaction goes away to be processed. Setting up standing orders is just as easy and payee details only need to be entered once, saving time on subsequent sessions.

Irritatingly, these transactions take place no more quickly than the old-fashioned paper versions. One institution quotes clearing times of up to five days on some transactions. So much for the new e-fficiency.

BARCLAYS

Barclays Bank Plc is, as they like to tell us, Big. Big, however does not imply nimble and quick-witted. Barclays' first attempt at Internet banking required users to use Barclays' proprietary client software as opposed to a browser. This proved unsatisfactory and now their customers can log on using their favourite browser, as long as it is the right version of Internet Explorer or Netscape Navigator.

Barclays' front page is well-designed and suitably elegant. All information you might need about online service is easy to find and not too slow to download. Account and transaction details can be downloaded in formats compatible with Microsoft Money 98 and 99 and spreadsheets (including Microsoft Excel).

Barclays is so keen to get customers that they are offering online services at no charge and advertising free Internet access (eg, no ISP fees) for life to all customers.

LLOYDSTSB

The front page of Lloyds TSB's iBanking site is a little more cluttered and less business-like than those of some of its rivals, with undue prominence given to their current special offers. The tone of their site seems to suggest that they are expecting many of their clients to be going online for the first time in order to take advantage of their Internet service.

Information is not clearly laid out and there is nothing resembling an in-depth FAQ that could be downloaded and read offline. Instead there is a very useful demo walkthrough of the transactions forms which are designed in a livery and shape suggestive of a Lloyd's chequebook. In use, the site is perfectly adequate and pages download quickly, despite a fair sprinkling of gifs. LloydsTSB do not have facilities to apply for an account online.

HONG-KONG SHANGHAI BANKING CORPORATION (HSBC)

HSBC arrived on UK high streets when the oriental giant swallowed the Midland Bank. The portal to their corporate site has a very international feel and has a comparatively diminutive link to their UK pages. The graphic design of the site is handsome and neat but a little gif-heavy which pushes up download times irritatingly.

Again, there is no consolidated FAQ instead there is an unwieldy and rather ostentatious Macromedia Flash demo-cum-walkthrough, which will give problems on older machines.

NATIONWIDE BUILDING SOCIETY

The Nationwide site differs little from its banker peers. The site is well-designed and the livery familiar to all existing customers. All pages download nice and quickly. Sign-up for Internet access to your account is straightforward and simple, despite the large number of details required. The form has a feature which can fill out your address for you just from your house number and post-code which is handy if you have forgotten where you live. It's a cool feature, though.

As might be expected, all the same functions are available to Nationwide customers as on the other sites.

It is most probable that the majority of people who are looking for Internet banking will be wanting to use the service with their existing bank account(s). This said, it is made perfectly easy by most banking web sites to apply to open a new account, either of a different kind with the same bank, or with an altogether new bank.

The HTML forms to be filled in are essentially the same as their paper counterparts. Again the process is no quicker than visiting a branch in person, since the bank will still need to check any required references and your credit history.

FIRST-E, AN INTERNET-ONLY BANK

As said, Internet banking represents lower overheads for banks but this does not necessarily benefit the consumer except in terms of convenience. What if a bank has no branches at all? First-e is just such a bank, offering current and savings accounts and most of the same services and facilities as the high-street banks. First-e promise to pass on the dividends of lowered overheads in the form of better interest rates on savings.

Accounts with First-e are opened over the Web on a secure server. Some details must still be sent physically as customers must provide a valid passport and two recent utilities bills to prove age, identity and address. The service is unavailable to certain foreign tax residents and those who only have a PO box postal address. First-e does not offer either joint or business accounts.

The bank's client software is compatible with Windows 9x and NT with Java enabled, but not Macintosh, Unix or OS/2 platforms at this time. An email address is also mandatory.

The instructions for sign-up suggest that the best way to open a First-e account is to transfer funds from your existing bank online but they include instructions as to how to have your bank make the arrangements for you. Cheques must be deposited by post, naturally, but this should not affect the time it takes for your money to clear.

Access to your hard-won cash is via a Maestro card. Chequebook, debit card and standing orders are all made available but First-e do not extend either an overdraft facility or a cheque guarantee card, so you can't go into the red. This is either a good thing or a bad thing dependent on your attitude to debt.

This could be the way that banks go in the future. Since forms may be filled in and funds shuffled from your PC, the only high-street presence a bank requires are the facilities to accept and dispense cash money. ATMs are already allowing us to access our cash from

First-e was the first Internet-only bank.

functionally non-aligned terminals. There is no reason why we might not, in the future, have mini 'bank malls' where small franchise-like offices service the needs of small traders and their cash takings.

BILL-PAYMENT COMPANIES

Bill-payment companies are a money-management service rather than credit or banking institutions. The idea is simple: you give the company as your billing address for all your regular bills and even one-off invoices. The company then pays your creditors on your behalf and sends you a single monthly bill for the whole lot plus a small management fee. The company will usually send you a statement such that you may approve all items to be paid. This saves you the hassle and paperwork that would need to be dealt with if you paid them all yourself. If it takes you an hour every month to pay your bills, and an hour of your time is worth more than £10, then it makes sense. If all you get are your utility bills along with a phone bill every quarter, then it is probably not for you.

There is nothing radically new about the idea but the use of the Internet has increased the speed and convenience with which the service can be accessed. Now, customers can view and track their bills at the payment company's site and authorize or refuse the issue of payments online.

Bill payment companies are very common in the US, mainly because, surprisingly, not all American banks yet support Electronic Funds Transfer (EFT). In the US, people use these services where in the UK people would be more likely to use a standing order or direct debit. Small businesses might rely on their accountant for the same thing.

Sole traders in the UK who must deal with a lot of suppliers' invoices etc. might well find this a viable and more economical solution.

BANKING ABROAD

The Internet banking situation varies from country to country although it is, of course, possible to have a bank account in a foreign country – especially online. Some ebanks, however, will specify that you must be a resident of a particular country before they will let you have an account with them. Generally you will find the usual USA/Europe divide. If you find a bank on the Internet that looks promising, don't forget to make sure that you are going to be able to use an account with them before wasting your time (and theirs) checking out other details like interest rates, etc.

GETTING A JOB

There may come a time when you need to change or find a real, traditional-style, 9–5 job. Although they say that 'you'll never get rich digging another man's ditch', it is sometimes necessary to do so while you save up for your own shovel.

Up until recently, there were a number of different avenues of research to be explored. There was the Jobcentre, newspaper ads, shop windows, cold-calling employers and trying your luck via the old boys' (or girls') network.

These methods all had something in common. First, you almost invariably had to stand up and go outdoors. Second, you usually had to look at hundreds of irrelevant ads before you found one suitably of interest to you. Third, no one out there was actually looking for you or, indeed, knew of your existence. Lastly, they were mostly a headache.

Well, all that has been changed by the advent of Internet recruitment services and job-search pages. No more must you wade through page after page of inappropriate ads. Everything is on the web now.

There are a number of different paths to employment on the World Wide Web but all tend to be quite similar in operation and may be centralized on one type of site. Below are described a few of the different types of sites that offer services to job-seekers. These services are usually free to the public, with fees charged to the advertisers.

JOB SITES

These are the equivalent of the jobs pages in any daily newspaper and, indeed, are often part of the Internet presence of the newspaper publishers themselves. The advantage that they have over their paper counterparts is the facility to search the vacancy database by a number of criteria such as type, area, salary band or keyword(s). Also, they may have useful links to specialist recruiters or to higher-profile vacancies.

GETTING A JOB

Additionally, in some cases, users can upload their CV to an employer-facing database, which recruiters pay for access to. You never know: you might be the one that all those corporate head-hunters are slavering after.

Some of these sites tactfully withhold your personal details until you decide to release them, which prevents your current boss from stumbling across your name whilst searching the CV database.

PEOPLEBANK.COM

Peoplebank offer two services to job-seekers. Without needing to register, it is possible simply to surf in and browse their searchable database of vacancies. The Peoplebank search form allows you

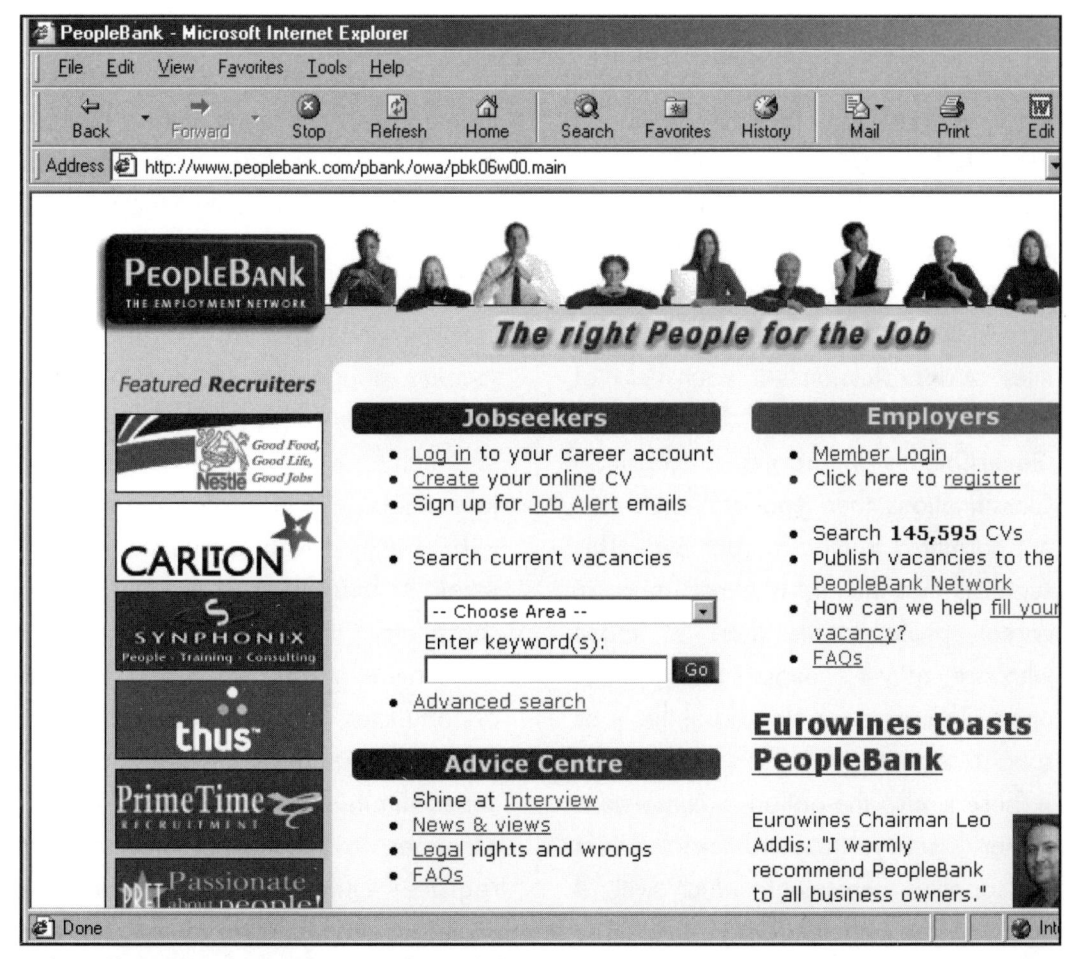

Find yourself a new job on the Internet – it's easier than you think.

to narrow the field of ads you look at by specifying a category (eg, media, IT&T – Information Technology and Telecoms – etc) and keywords to be viewed.

By registering, which is as easy as entering your name and date of birth and choosing a password, users can fill in a CV form. To integrate it with their search engine more easily, Peoplebank insist on an HTML form being filled out rather than accepting uploaded word processor files. While it is easy enough to cut and paste from a text document on your desktop, which is fine for your hobbies and interests, the employment history section is quite restrictive. Job category and title must be selected from drop-down menus with closed lists of job titles and professions. If your field of expertise is not included in the Government's Standard Occupation Classifications then you are stuck and not permitted to type in your own. This suggests that the site is aimed more at career professionals than at those who are, as yet, 'keeping their options open'. The same can be said of the 'jobs sought' section.

There is also the option to complete a rather scary psychometric quiz (personality assessment) which will, if you wish, be appended to your CV. The test results are not automatically available to you unless requested. The test is scary because it is a multiple-choice affair with no 'none of the above' answers permitted. Peoplebank assure us that there are no wrong answers but whether the idea appeals to you depends largely on your attitude to psychometry in general.

JOBSUNLIMITED.COM

JobsUnlimited is part of the Internet arm of the *Guardian* and *Observer* newspapers. It is worth noting that not every ad that appears on the site database will necessarily be duplicated in the paper version or vice-versa.

The front page has many links to services and featured vacancies from recruitment agencies, along with links to other services for job-seekers on the site. A search form allows direct access to the jobs database or you can dive straight in to browse by categories like media, IT&T, legal & finance, new media, public sector etc. Other links lead to sections and feature articles on courses, graduate opportunities, charities and so on.

An outstanding feature of the JobsUnlimited site is the Career Manager. To use this it is necessary to register. Once set up, the Career Manager can be programmed to search the database on a daily basis for specified keywords and phrases. A number of independent searches can be set up this way. Next time you log in, your Career Manager will already have ferreted out the jobs of interest to you.

Jobs Unlimited do not accept CVs.

BIGBLUEDOG.COM

Though its name is crashingly irrelevant and fatuous, this outgrowth of Associated Newspapers (*Evening Standard*, *Metro* etc.) is not dissimilar to its rivals. The front page is headed by a nifty search form which allows four criteria to be chosen: job type, salary, location and keyword(s), before a final click sets the query in motion.

Other links lead to feature articles pages that will already be familiar to regular readers of Associated's publications. There is also a CV submission form. If this looks eerily similar to the one at Peoplebank, that's because it is. In fact, the BigBlueDog CV feature is operated by Peoplebank and submitted CVs will also appear on the Peoplebank site.

There appears, compared to other sites, a preponderance of telesales and callcentre-type jobs here.

CV SUBMISSION SITES

These work slightly differently to the Jobsearch sites, though there is a degree of overlap. While some sites do have searchable databases of vacancies, their primary mode of operation is to match your CV with an employer's requirements, then inform the user of the vacancy.

Probably due to the extra work and individual attention that this requires, CV submission sites tend to restrict their scope to one professional field. Such sites tend to be more sober in their presentation, lacking the frills, features and profusion of links found on other jobsearch sites.

CBS APPOINTMENTS

CBS are a technical recruitment specialist. They maintain a searchable database of IT&T (Information Technology and Telecoms) and engineering vacancies, both contract and permanent.

CBS accept CVs in 'all major word-processor formats' so users are not restricted in their descriptions of their employment history by the narrow definitions of the Standard Occupation Classifications.

JOBDIRECT

JobDirect also has a keyword-searchable database. This CV submission service matches your CV to the stated requirements of employers and forwards details of the vacancy to the job-seekers that best match the requirements.

Similar to JobsUnlimited's Career Manager, JobDirect can be programmed to find ads that conform to your criteria and email them to you automatically and at no charge. CVs to be made available to employers are accepted in a number of formats.

OTHER OPPORTUNITIES

Another good place to look for jobs is on the pages of prospective employers' websites. This is the Internet equivalent of help-wanted ads in high-street shop windows, only more upmarket. Many companies now advertise their current vacancies on their homepages. So, if you have a specific desire to work at, say, Dixons or PC World, just go to their site and you are likely to find a link from the index (front) page to their personnel and recruitment department.

Even if there are no links or job ads in evidence on a corporate site, it might even be worth using the ubiquitous 'enquiries' link to contact their personnel department. Some employers may be impressed by a proactive approach like this. If you are convinced that the job you want is with them, give it a go.

PERSONAL PROMOTION VIA INFO SITES

So, surfing the ads and hawking your CV around the World Wide Web is all very well, but even the humblest megabyte of server space on your domestic account homepage can be made to work for you.

A homepage can be used to give far more expansive and detailed information about yourself, your interests and your achievements than is appropriate in a business-like CV. With your creativity unfettered and your imagination unleashed, you can display examples of your best work, be it in text, pictures, video or music format. Artists and graphics designers can post scans of their work, writers can publish their musings. A hairstylist could persuade their comeliest customers to pose for testimonial pictures, performers could upload clips from their show-reel… whatever you do, there is a way of showing off on the web. HTML coders can really go to town. A facial photo is not out of place, provided that you are not objectionably ugly. There is always Photoshop to fall back on for acne and tattoo removal.

Using a homepage to advertise your employability must be addressed seriously. A badly designed or (gasp) faulty site with broken links and missing images will be off-putting to anyone who wants to be impressed by your attention to detail and ability to organize and present information clearly. Though you have much more latitude and freedom to be expressive than in a CV, take care not to get carried away and do filter your sense of humour carefully. While the tone you are aiming for will be dependent upon the employers you wish to impress, think of it more as a corporate presentation than as a gallery of your holiday snaps. The odd family photo, however, may appeal to bosses who are looking for stable, family types.

Think of the web site as an extended version of your CV and lay it out as such with different pages for the different categories of information about yourself. Enlarge upon the information given in your CV. For example, when discussing your previous jobs, describe what you enjoyed most about each. Resist the temptation to criticize past employers – stay upbeat and positive. Use this as an opportunity for a bit of relaxed and chatty self-promotion. You can also have a conventional version of your CV ready for anyone to download. If you do this, take care to use a file format that everyone can read: either a simple text file, or a Microsoft Word document.

Corporate head-hunters and other prospective employers are only likely to surf on to your site by the bizarrest of accidents, so, how do you strut your stuff for the people who matter?

You could try including your job-seeking credentials in the index page and metatags of your web site, so that any search engines or directories that you submit your URL to will return your page as a result should anyone be trying to fill vacancies through a search engine. This is probably not going to get you far in reality. Really the only viable method is to make sure that your URL is displayed among the contact details on your CV and in any emails you might send. This way it can backup and enhance your CV, though it is improbable that it will be visited unless you have already been shortlisted. If you have it could make the difference between an interview and a 'no thanks'.

Always make sure that the contents of both CV and homepage are in accord and that they are synchronized regularly.

PREPARING A GOOD CV

There are a great many places where you can go for tips and advice on how best to write your CV. There will be books at your nearest library, and the governmental job agencies always claim to offer advice on the subject.

Much more convenient, when you are already at your word processor (which may have a handy CV wizard installed) are the online tips pages to be found on many jobsearch web sites. Given that it is inappropriate to duplicate their content here, the essentials are as follows:

CVs should err more on the side of staid-ness, and should never be flashy. Always use a sans serif font, like Arial. Colours, if you must use them, should be kept to a minimum and not much more garish than navy blue. Use good quality paper of no less than 100 gsm quality. Any colour paper you like, as long as it's white, though some say that cream is acceptable and may make your CV stand out in a heap on someone's desk. As long as no one else uses cream paper, of course.

A typical CV should come out at around two pages, dependent on your age and experience. It should consist of five main headings:

- Personal and contact details – ie, name, nationality, date of birth, address, phone, fax, email, URL etc.
- Education and training – in reverse chronological order.
- Career and work history – in reverse chronological order. Including your rôle within the company, your responsibilities, the skills you used and acquired. Remember that misdeclaring experience on your CV is now counted as fraud.
- Prior positions of responsibility – not necessarily in the workplace. Could include positions in student clubs or societies.
- Your hobbies and interests – your activities outside work. As a rule, 'socialising' and 'watching TV' are unimpressive and should not be included. Don't overembellish. You may have to back up your claims later at interview.

As a rule of thumb, it is the first sections that win you an interview and the latter sections that give you something to talk about when you are there. The purpose of an interview is not only to confirm your professional credentials but also to have the opportunity to assess whether your personality is suitable to the company or office you will be working in.

Information should be presented as short, bullet-pointed statements. Key points are best emphasized by isolating them with surrounding white space (ie, two carriage-returns before and after the paragraph), rather than using bold text. You can edit your CV strategically for each application to re-emphasize the qualities specified in the job advertisement.

Then, check, double-check and check again before asking someone else to proof-read it for you. If there is nothing else to choose between two applicants, they will pick the one who can spell. It is best to use an A4 envelope if you are posting your CV snail-mail since you do not want to have to fold and crease your masterpiece.

In this electronic age, many of your applications may be sent via email. It is easy to send a word processor file as an attachment but you cannot rely on the recipient having the same word processor as yourself. What if you use a PC and they have Macs? While Macintoshes are smart enough to read Windows files in most cases, the opposite is not true. If people can't open the file first time, they may simply file you under 'recycle' there and then. Plain text is an option but will be the very death of all your exquisite formatting. A good solution to this is to paste the text into an HTML editor like Dreamweaver and format it there. An HTML document can be read in and printed from their email client software regardless of platform or operating system. A bonus is that you can insert hyperlinks to relevant portions of your web page if you have one. Make sure your pages are in good order first! Internal hyperlinks ('bookmarks' in some editors) can be included at the top of the page which take the reader directly to the sub-heading of their choice. Do not be tempted by clip-art or anything fancy, just because it is in HTML. Such things will only annoy people. Keep it simple and keep it small so that people won't have to wait ages for your application or your CV to download.

COVERING LETTERS

Some applications must be made via a company's application form – usually to be posted back accompanied by your CV. Where this is not the case, a covering letter will be required. This letter will tie your CV to a particular vacancy as the company may be advertising several. When there are a large number of applicants sending CVs, a good covering letter may be the only thing that gets your CV read. A weak one could see your best efforts binned, unread. Do not use a fill-in-the-blanks type stock letter – they stand out a mile. Write a new one specifically for each application. Use this chance to emphasize the qualities which you feel you have to offer this employer in particular.

The guidelines are:

- The text must, of course, be perfect in terms of grammar and spelling.
- Know who you are writing to, their title and position. Are they the personnel manager or your prospective boss?
- Write in your own words; try not to sound like you have copied from a book.
- Know about the firm and what they do.
- Use the employer's language and frame of reference where possible.
- Address the requirements stated in the ad and how you meet them.
- Important points can be emphasized in **bold** text.

In the end, wherever you find a job that you want, a well presented CV and covering letter are the most important part of a successful application. Remember that yours will be one of a great many that flood in, especially for the coolest of jobs.

Your CV has to stand out from all of the others without the aid of gimmicks like coloured paper or ink, which will get it binned. The best way to do this within the limited scope which is available to you is to perfect the layout in such a way that the skills which suit you to the job will catch the reader's eye. If you have friends who work in graphic design, ask them to give your CV a once-over to make sure that it looks good. You could even look in your local library for advice about laying a document out — it can make a difference!

ONLINE AUCTIONS

People have been getting rid of stuff they don't want in more creative ways than just sticking it in the bin for years. There are jumble sales, car boot sales, charity shops or even the small ads in the local paper. The problem with these is that they are often time-consuming and offer little opportunity to drive up the price you get for your unwanted goods.

Fortunately for the financially minded, the Internet has brought us another option: online auctions. These work in much the same way as a conventional auction. You put an item up for sale, people bid on it, and the highest bidder secures the item, buying it for the price of their bid.

The advantage of using an Internet auction site is that suddenly your auction room becomes everyone on the Internet, not just a few people in the sale room of a traditional auction house.

Interestingly, the success of online auctions has been great enough that the physical-world auction houses are beginning to take notice. Many homes and commercial properties are already sold by auction, if the owner wants a quick and easy sale. The first of a breed of property auction sites on the Internet have started to appear, and more are due to follow (see Chapter 20).

There are some differences between the two forms of auction, though. For one, Internet sales do not stop after the highest bid is extracted from the room. Because bidders can join the auction at any time, the sale continues for a set period of time, and the highest bid by the end of that time wins the goods.

Unlike real-world auctions, the stuff you sell on the internet doesn't have to be valuable, unusual or collectible: it just has to be something other people might want. You can register pretty much anything you want to sell, with a few restrictions discussed below, and hopefully at the end of the auction period you've got rid of your stuff.

With a bit of luck, there will have been enough interest in the item that people ended up bidding against each other. Just as in physical auction houses, that's the route to really big money for goods. Many buyers get carried away by the competitive feel of the bidding process, driving the sale price well above what they would otherwise have been prepared to pay.

BUYING FOR ENTERTAINMENT

Indeed, auction sites seem to generate a definite buzz, so people end up bidding on the most unusual items, things they never realized they wanted. The act of taking part in the auction is part of the fun for some users, and the acquisition of the item at the end of it is almost incidental. All of which, of course, is good news for sellers.

Of course, selling old stuff isn't the only way of making money out of these auction sites. They can also be used as a sales channel for carefully selected items, and many people do just that. If you have a reasonable knowledge of what is collectible in a particular field, then you can make money by buying things to auction later, in the hope that the competition among potential buyers will at some point in the near future drive the price much higher than that which you paid for it.

Viewing things from the buyer's perspective, auction sites can be great for getting second-hand goods cheap. If you're after something specific – a book, a peripheral for your computer, a CD and so on – try bidding for it on an auction site. As long as you keep in mind its original cost, you can save significant amounts of money this way.

However, the first thing potential buyers have to do is find something they want, which is sometimes less easy than it seems. There are several ways of doing it. If the buyer is after something in particular, they do a search on it using the search facility most of the auction web sites offer. This will throw up anything relevant plus some only vaguely related goods. Otherwise all the auction sites divide the goods on offer into different categories and sub-categories. The prospective buyer can click their way through the various categories the site is subdivided into, down to the individual category and then the items on offer within it.

Once they choose an item they are interested in, they can place a bid. The web site will require them to register, and usually to provide credit card details, before they can start bidding.

Placing a bid is simplicity itself, which is one of the reasons the sites are so popular. You just type in the amount you are bidding, sign in with your user name and password and within seconds the bid is logged on the site.

BID AND COUNTER-BID

Over the next week, or however long the auction runs for, prospective buyers need to monitor the auction, and if a higher bid is placed, up their own bid. Luckily there are several ways of making this easier. Some web sites allow buyers to monitor an auction they are interested in. Whenever a higher bid is placed, the site contacts them by email or mobile phone SMS message. Some browser software also monitors auctions whenever you go online. Recent versions of Microsoft Internet Explorer have this ability. It alerts you with a distinctive sound when it discovers that an auction has changed since you last looked at it.

Another option, on some sites, is to put in your bid and then specify the maximum bid you are prepared to make. Then it allows the site itself to automatically up the bid whenever anyone else outbids you. The site will keep doing this until your maximum bid is reached, notifying you as it does so.

Waiting until the last moment to make your bid is not always a good idea. Some sites have a hierarchy of winners, to determine who gets the lot. Obviously, the person who bids the most wins. However, sometimes a bidder who is using the automatic bidding feature described above in use will be allowed to up his or her bid to match the new highest bid. Their bid is then given priority because they were the earliest of the two bidders to join the sale. Another condition sometimes used to determine the winner in this situation is that whoever bids for the most amount of items wins. Some sales can be of a group of items and the auctioning site lets you bid on only some of them, if you wish.

GETTING THE GOODS

Once the buyer has won their auction, they must get in touch with the seller via email to arrange the exchange of goods and, most importantly, money. Once the seller has provided a postal address, they send off payment and wait for their goods to return in the post.

Sellers have plenty of options when auctioning an item. Every site requires you to register your details: name, address, contact information and usually a credit card number. The last bit of information is used for charging you for listing your items on the site – the auction web sites aren't charities, they're businesses in their own right.

First of all, you have to select which category your item fits into. It is important to get this right. If your goods are in the wrong, or the least obvious, category, they are less likely to attract bids. Equally, a good, accurate and exciting description of the item on sale is vitally important in drawing people's attention to that particular auction.

PRIVATE VIEWING

Some sites offer you the option to include a photograph of the item for sale. This can be a useful opportunity if the item is something that looks interesting. A good photograph will also give the buyer an idea of the condition of the item you are selling. For some collectors, this is a very important factor and you can considerably boost your chances of getting a good price from your auction by demonstrating that your wares are in top condition.

You may well have the option to set a minimum price you are willing to accept: a reserve price below which the goods will not be sold. If you are aiming to sell goods at a profit, rather than just dispose of old junk, this is a vital option. Set it at a level that gives you a clear profit margin, but not a huge one. However, your reserve price does not need to be your minimum first bid: it's often better to set a minimum bid that's below your reserve price to attract bidders into the auction who might be put off by the true, reserve price. Once the bidding starts, they often forget their initial reticence as they struggle to beat those people who are outbidding them.

You can also, on some sites, set the bid increment. This specifies the minimum amount each bidder is allowed to increase their bid by. The level you choose to set this at will depend on the worth of the item you're selling. If the total value of the auction is in the hundreds of pounds or dollars, it makes sense to have a bid increment in the tens of the currency. However, if the item is only expected to fetch a few pounds, a bid increment of between 10p and 50p makes more sense. Again, choosing too high a bid increment will put some bidders off, which is not to your benefit.

The down side to many of these extra options is that they cost you money. Most of the auction sites will charge you some money just for listing your goods on the sites. Then, they will take a percentage of the amount of money you make through selling the item. Many of these additional costs will push the price of selling the goods up even higher, so ask yourself carefully whether the potential sale price is worth the extra promotion you are putting behind it. If the answer is no, stick to the basic listing.

You then choose the length of time the action will run for: this is usually between a week and ten days. A longer period gives buyers more time to find the auction, while a shorter period might lead to more frenzied bidding as the deadline approaches faster.

THE WAITING GAME

Once these choices are made, you start the auction and wait. While it's very easy to monitor the auction by visiting the web site, there is very little you can do. Some sites allow buyers to email questions to the sellers. If you do get a question, do your best to answer it honestly. There's no point in lying: virtually every site has a provision for buyers to complain about mis-sold goods. Some even allows buyers to comment on sellers, ruining your chances of ever selling again through that site if you are caught being dishonest.

There are other ways you can promote what you are selling, though. You can usually post brief details of a sale to mailing lists or Internet newsgroups that deal with the sort of goods you are selling, to try and drive more people to the sale. Including the URL of the sale itself in the email is probably a good idea. It makes it much simpler for people to find your item. However, be careful before doing this. Some newsgroups and mailing lists have rules against this sort of advertising, and if you break them you may find yourself thrown off the list or, worse, 'flamed' – which means that you will find your email inbox full of angry messages from users of that group.

Once the bidding period has passed, you will be notified of the winner by email or by SMS message on your mobile phone, depending on the method you chose when the auction was set up. Of course, there's a chance that no-one will bid on the item, or that your reserve price won't be met. In that case, you'll be told that you have failed to find a buyer and your credit card will be charged for the listing fee, and any further advertising you selected, but not for a commission fee.

If you have successfully sold your item, you then need to negotiate with the buyer about how you are going to get the item to them. The first question is who pays postage. Obviously, if you are a buyer you want the seller to pay and if you are the seller, you want the buyer to do it!

The best way to sort this out is to decide before the auction happens. Most auction sites allow the seller to specify who pays for the postage, allowing potential buyers to make allowance for that when they place their bids and decide how high they can afford to go. On a large item, the postage can significantly add to the cost of the purchase.

When working out postage, don't forget to factor in the cost of decent packaging. Both sides want the goods to arrive in good shape, and protective packaging isn't always cheap. If your buyer has agreed to pay postage for his goods, be sure to check with him the level of postage he's prepared to support. While a postage box filled with packaging material and registered delivery might be the safest option, it might be outside his price range.

Of course, if the buyer lives locally, it might be easier to meet in person to exchange the goods, just as you would if you sold something through a newspaper's small ads. As always when meeting people you met through the Internet, play safe: meet in a public place and make sure friends known where you are and who you are with.

In most cases, though, you will end up posting the goods. There are some significant risks here: if you dispatch your goods before payment has arrived, or before the cheque has cleared, then you run the risk of having surrendered your possessions to a dishonest user of the auction sites.

CAVEAT EMPTOR

Buyers can attempt to defraud you in other ways, too. They could claim that the item never arrived. You can make that less likely by sending the item in a manner that requires a signature upon delivery, but that again will add to the cost of posting it.

Most sites attempt to solve this problem by acting as middlemen in the process. Some sites store either payment or goods, until both have been received, than forward them on to the relevant parties. Others take payment and hold it as bond until they hear that the goods have arrived safely. However, most sites charge a fee for these services, so they may well not be economic for small sales. For bigger sales, these services are a useful safeguard against fraud.

If the auction site has a rating system, and your buyer has used the site before, you may be able to get some idea of their trustworthiness from the comments other sellers have made. If there are no comments or they are a first-time buyer, you will just have to take a risk.

There are restrictions on the types of goods you can sell using Internet auctions. Obviously illegal material like drugs and hardcore pornography are clearly and comprehensively banned by every web site – even aside from the fact that it is illegal under UK law to sell these items. Advertising the fact that you are selling such goods on a public forum like an online auction house is as good a way as any to guarantee a visit by the police to your home for a little chat about the relevant legislation, and how it will affect your court case. Most sites even ban the sale of softcore pornography, even if it can legally be

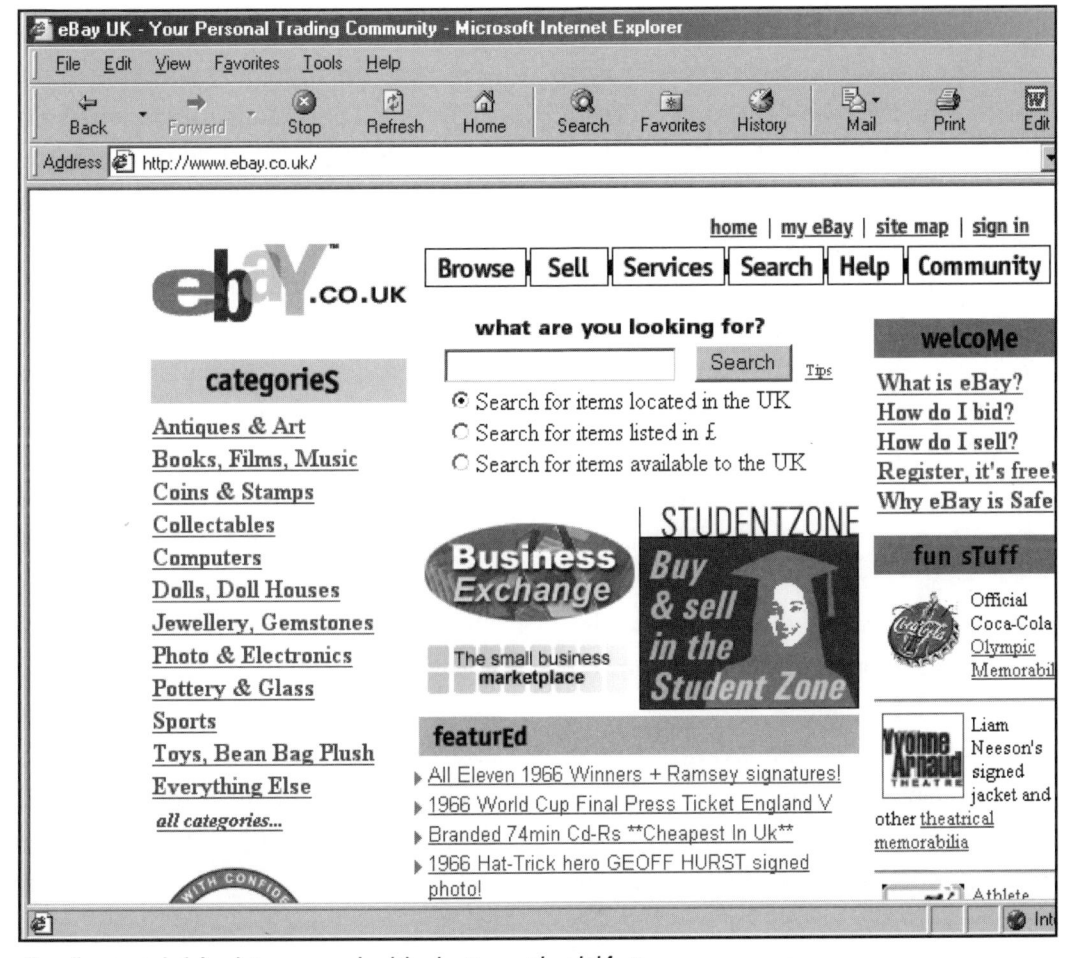

Ebay allows you to look for whatever you need and then buy it – or at least bid for it.

sold in the country you are in.

The same restrictions usually apply to firearms and other weapons. Even if their sale is legal in the UK, many sites choose to ban them. Better to be safe than sorry in their eyes. The scandal attached to selling an item which was then used in a crime would be enough to destroy a web site's credibility.

Some web sites, like eBay, have several international versions. They often allow you to sell and buy items on some or all of the sites simultaneously. There's no doubt that this can be a big advantage. For the buyer, it broadens the range of goods you have access to. Some items which aren't available in the UK may well be on sale elsewhere in the world. There's even a chance of bagging something much cheaper abroad than you would ever get it at home. However, you have to keep track of exchange rates, to make sure you are getting a good deal. Getting money to the seller can be a problem if they won't use the web site's systems, and postage can be expensive and painfully slow.

From the seller's point of view, it opens up the sale to a world audience. The more buyers, the higher the chance of finding interested bidders, and the greater the competition for a particular item is likely to be. That may well boost the price you get for an item far higher than a single-country auction will be able to.

However, before you leap into international auctioneering there are some major pitfalls to consider, too. Firstly, postage costs rocket once you start sending goods of any size internationally. This quickly cuts into your profit margins or savings from buying the object in an auction.

As a seller, you could specify that the buyer will pay postage, but that runs the risk of driving away potential bidders. Once again, the size and worth of the item on offer is a key factor. A small, therefore cheap to post, item of high worth is probably the ideal international sell in postage cost terms. Its postage cost is a small enough proportion of the overall price that it is not an issue.

However, even if an acceptable postage agreement is reached, there are other complications. First of all, the country you are sending to may well impose some sort of tax on the import of certain goods. If so, you have to establish with the buyer who will be responsible for payment of these fees. While this is not a big problem within the European Union, where free trade agreements have virtually done away with restrictions on trade between member countries, exports to the US and other countries do run the risk of falling foul of local customs laws.

Then there are the complex problems involved in transferring money. Most banks will accept cheques drawn in a foreign currency, but will charge you a hefty fee for doing so. Using a credit card-based scheme run by the web site itself is probably the best solution to this problem.

More seriously, the import of certain goods may be forbidden by other countries. While the obvious suspects like pornography and firearms aren't usually sold on auction sites, some less obvious candidates might be restricted. For example, many countries have a ban on the import of seeds.

FROM FOREIGN LANDS

If you are buying from abroad, the same problems apply. Even if you find a site that will sell you pornography or weapons, there's no guarantee that customs will let them through. Indeed, an attempt to bring them in might lead to unwelcome attention from customs officials or even the police.

Even less obviously problematic goods carry a risk. Many goods might be subjects to extra tax when you bring them into the country, especially if you have bought several items. If you aren't aware of this in advance, you may find the price of your purchase leaping beyond the point where it was a good deal.

So what should you sell? The simple answer is pretty much anything that is in reasonable condition and is still usable. Buyers come to the site for all sorts of reasons, from trying to acquire specific items for a collection, to buying household goods cheap, to just participating because auctions are fun.

Jewellery, electrical items, books, CDs and video and other household items dominate most sites. Everyone needs and wants them, most people have examples of them they don't want, so it's easy to see why they have become the backbone of the web sites' trading.

Computer goods are common, too, given that a high proportion of the user base is very IT-literate. Anything from redundant games to pieces of hardware, including complete computer systems that sellers no longer need can be found on the web, and can be yours in ten days for the right price.

Some goods will get higher prices than others. Unique and rare goods are a really good way of getting a high price and use the 'suction' format to its best. Something autographed by a celebrity, film star or other well-known figure attracts lots of bidders.

Anything which is collectible is also a good bet – collectors are willing to pay highly for something they prize. Old memorabilia from films and television programmes is always popular and stands a good chance of getting a high price.

However, there are some goods which struggle to sell. Many people use auction web sites as ways of unloading redundant vinyl LPs and cassettes, which have been replaced by CDs, minidiscs or even MP3 files. As a result, several of the sites are swamped by old vinyl records that very few people want any more. Unless the album is rare, collectible, or doesn't exist as a CD, you don't have a great chance of selling it, let alone getting a good price for it. However, if you're willing to take a small price for it, or even a nominal price, it is a viable way of disposing of these goods.

Equally, CDs are common enough that it is difficult to get a good price. However, if you're just looking to dispose of an unwanted gift or a CD whose appeal has paled, it will make you more money than the charity shop will. Of course, a rare CD stands a good chance of attracting high bids, like any rare goods. This is especially true if the album has been deleted, making an online auction one of the few easy ways someone can get hold of it.

The same applies to videos. If that particular cassette is freely available in the shops, you can only expect to sell it as a bargain, at a significant discount to the original price. Disney videos, which are often released for limited periods and then deleted for a decade or more, are a good bet and attract enthusiastic bidding.

Do not restrict yourself to personal items, either. Business goods are often auctioned on the sites. It's an efficient way for small enterprises to dispose of unwanted equipment or to acquire it cheaply. Some businesses produce goods to be auctioned on these web sites, finding it a cheap and efficient way of marketing their business and its products.

TOP SITES
http://www.ebay.co.uk

Probably the best-known of all the auction sites. eBay is a major player in online auctioning internationally and probably your first choice if you want to sell overseas as well as in the UK. EBay has other, international, sites that are all accessible from each other. Check for your country in the lists and decide if you want a 'local' or international sale or purchase. Remember to follow the criteria stated above.

http://auctions.yahoo.co.uk

Is there anything Yahoo! doesn't do? The site is not particularly exciting, but is quick and efficient, and has a good user base. There's a special celebrity auction section, for the star-struck looking to acquire or sell a piece of their hero's life.

This site again has international versions so make sure you are buying/selling from to prospective sellers/purchasers in the right part of the world.

http://www.firedup.com

Firedup is a relatively new entrant to the field of the online auction. It was launched with a big bang on the back of a really big advertising budget featuring Hollywood superstar Bruce Willis. How much of an impact it will make in a

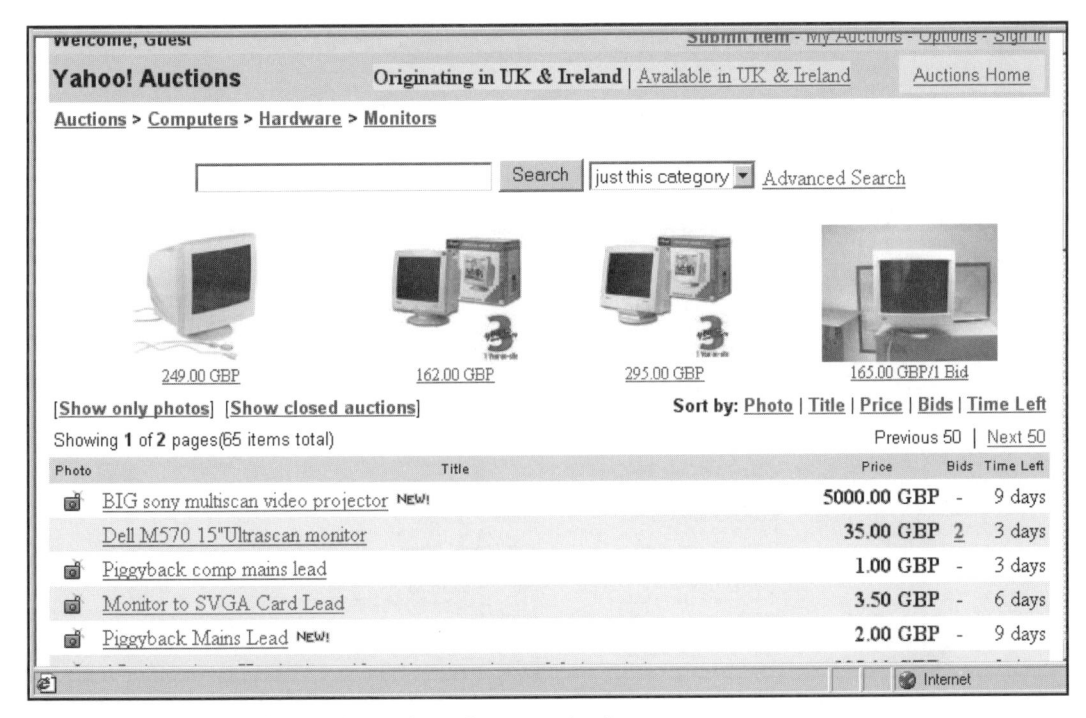

Yahoo! runs auctions – another feather in the cap of a very busy Internet-based company.

crowded marketplace remains to be seen. Mainly a North American market, it is, of course, open to people from around the world.

http://www.qxl.com

A UK-launched site, set up by a former newspaper journalist. The QXL stands for Quick Sell, believe it or not. The site's recent redesign has made using it much, much easier.

http://www.fsauctions.co.uk

Freeserve, the UK's largest Internet Service Provider, has also joined the auctioning game. If you are based in England, or are an anglophile, it is definitely worth a look because of the large number of British web users who have easy access to it. Being attached to Freeserve ensures the popularity of this site, in the way that Yahoo's ensures its own as well.

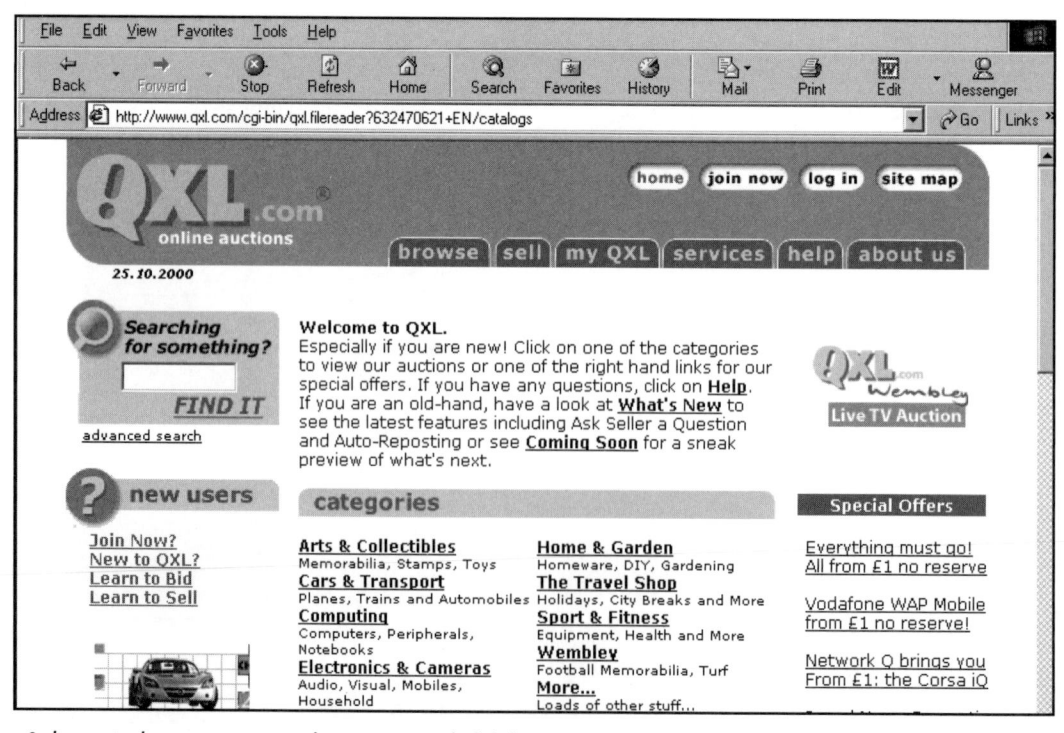

On-line auction houses are gaining popularity on a seemingly daily basis.

BUYING AND SELLING SHARES

To some people the thrill of the stock market is one of the biggest highs. To others it just means a scary scenario where young men in suits shout across a crowded room as fortunes are made and lost, and reputations are staked. In reality, the world of share-dealing is quite simple and can, if you are willing to put in a little research, be highly lucrative. Add in the World Wide Web and you could be laughing.

There's no doubt that share-dealing in the City is seen as one of the surest ways to make big amounts of money – or to lose it. The tail end of the 1980s was full of stories of yuppies earning vast fortunes in the share markets. The early 1990s was full of tales of losing it.

Share-dealing has never been very accessible to the general public. Those yuppies making the money were usually employed by one of the big city banks or trading houses, and made their money by buying and selling with other people's money. Simply put, unless you had vast sums of money to invest so one of these traders could do the share-dealing for you, you had little or no chance of actually doing anything significant with the stock markets.

Several years ago, there was an attempt to bring share ownership to the masses, with the flotation of the public utilities. It never came to much though. Despite several banks setting up specialist share-dealing services through local branches, it was still hard for the public to play the markets effectively.

The Internet has changed all that. The growth of web sites allowing you to trade shares online has made the same kind of quick trading for profitability feasible to the small investor, as long as they have regular access to the Internet.

How, though, do shares work, and how do you make money by buying and selling them?

Shares are nothing more than a small part of the ownership of a company. Private companies are owned either by an individual or by a small group of people. Public companies are owned by thousands of people, who have a varying number of shares in that company. These shares entitle the shareholders to a say in the running of the company, through a meeting, usually known as the Annual General Meeting. There, they can vote on issues related to the company and thus influence the decisions made by the board of directors. They also earn a share of the company's profits, called a dividend.

Not many people get rich through dividends alone, unless they have a large shareholding to start with. So, how do people make money from shares? Shares are bought or sold on a stock exchange. There are many of these all over the world. The best-known of them in the UK is the London Stock Exchange. However, there are others including the Alternative Investment Market (AIM) and many more abroad.

When people want to buy or sell shares in a company, they go through the stock markets. Prices are set on the basis of supply and demand. If a lot of people want to buy shares in a particular stock, the price will go up. If a lot of people are trying to get rid of their shares in that company, the prices will drop rapidly, because there is a glut of them available.

BUY OR SELL?

The decision to sell or buy a stock can be driven by any number of things. If a company announces a bad set of financial results, or warns of a forthcoming drop in its profits, many people will try and sell their shares quickly, before the price drops too far. On the other hand, an announcement by the company that it has launched a new product that people feel will boost its success will result in a rise in the share price, as people buy stock in the hope of seeing further rises as the business improves. An announcement by one company that it is going to try to buy a majority stake in another company through buying its shares will often drive up the share price of the company under threat, because people hope the would-be buyer will offer them an even higher figure for their shares or their support.

To make money in the short term appears simple. You have to buy shares in a particular company while its price is low, and then sell when the share price rises. The difference between the two is your profit. For example, a trader buys 1,000 shares in NewITCompany Ltd, a recent flotation on the stock market. Its shares are cheap at the moment, only 50p each, so the investor has only spent £500. However, the company makes an announcement of a deal to supply a major international chemicals company with hardware worldwide and suddenly the share price rockets to £2. The investor decides to take his money and run, selling the shares for £2,000, compared to his original investment of £500.

While this appears to be a simple idea, the actual execution of it isn't. It is very hard to judge whether the value of a share will go up or down without inside knowledge about the company's trading position, or knowledge of a forthcoming take-over bid. Thus, trading in this way is a matter of informed guesswork. Of course, you always run the risk of seeing the shares you have bought plunge disastrously in value, reducing the value of your investment significantly.

One way to lessen the risk is to buy for the long term rather than the short term. Here, you buy shares with the intention of keeping them for a long time, looking only to get a profit at the end. With this sort of investment, the short-term ups and downs of the shares aren't a major issue. The investor is looking to make money through a steady, long-term growth in the company's average share price.

In the previous example, say that despite the sudden growth in the company's share price, the investor reckons that the company will grow for several years yet and that the share price will continue to grow. So, he hangs on to his shares, hoping for a bigger pay-off in a couple of years. In the meantime, he enjoys a steady flow of dividends from the profits the company is making from the chemicals company contract. However, even that is not guaranteed, as poor profits can result in poor or non-existent dividends.

Company shares aren't the only things you can trade in the hope of making a profit. The currency markets are another arena for this sophisticated financial gambling. All currencies have an exchange rate with other currencies, which varies over time just as share prices do, and for similar reasons. The more demand there is for one particular type of currency to be converted into another country's currency, the higher that currency's exchange rate goes. Equally, if no-one is interested in buying a particular currency, the exchange rate plummets.

Many factors can affect these rates. One is the general economic health of a nation. Usually, the better the country is doing as a whole, the higher the exchange rate. Another major factor is bank interest rates. People like to invest their money in the currencies of countries with high bank interest rates, so their cash grows faster between trades. So if a country's interest rate is high, its currency becomes expensive to purchase.

Traders make money by buying lots of a particular currency when the exchange rate is high. For example, a British trader could convert a lot of her pounds into dollars when the exchange rate is high: for example, suppose she had £1,000 and the exchange rate was 1.7, she would end up with $1,700. Now, if the exchange rate were to drop to 1.4, she could convert her dollars back into pounds, giving her nearly £1,215 – a profit of over 20 per cent. By constantly switching between different currencies, she can continue to grow that particular pot of money.

MORE COMPLICATIONS

People also trade on the futures exchanges, including the London International Financial Futures Exchange (LIFFE). This is a slightly more complex idea. It is a contract, rather than something you physically purchase. Normally, it relates to the purchase and sale of a particular type of goods at a set price at a set date in the future, although it can also relate to other things, like particular financial services or instruments. Futures contracts came about as a safeguard. They allowed people who regularly buy and sell particular kinds of goods to insulate themselves against changes in the price of those goods.

In essence, if a company knows it will have a large consignment of a particular type of goods, say coffee, for sale in a few months' time, it can do one of two things. The company can wait until it takes delivery of the goods, and then sell them at the going rate then. This doesn't suit many companies, because they like to know exactly what their income will be as far in advance as possible to aid in planning. To avoid this problem, the company can take the second option and fix the consignment of coffee at the current price and sell a futures contract.

This works for the buyers, such as supermarket, too. They too like to plan their financial outgoings, so they can buy their coffee supply for three months time at today's prices.

Not surprisingly, manufacturers and consumers aren't the only people who get involved in this game. Speculators often buy futures contracts in the hope of selling them to a needy consumer at a later point for a higher price, increasing their profit.

Before the advent of the Internet, you had to use brokers to do these sales for you. You would either instruct them to buy or sell shares, futures or currency on an individual basis, or invest a sum of money – usually a large one – in a portfolio of varied shares, or even different types of financial products. They would then manage these with the aim of producing long-term growth. For most individuals, the second option was preferable to the first, because it required less time and effort to maintain. The brokers made their money by charging commission on each transaction, or a fee for managing the portfolio.

Internet share-dealing sites have altered this situation. By setting themselves up as virtual brokers, they allow you to buy and sell shares quickly from your computer. In fact, they give you access to transactions nearly as fast as the stockbrokers can manage using their own computer trading systems.

First of all, you have to open an account with a particular online broker, so shop around. There are more and more people now competing for your business. Some are specialized Internet brokers whose business is entirely on-line. Others are existing brokers or banks who are offering online brokerage as an extra service. A list of some of them can be found at the end of the chapter, but new players are entering the market all the time.

You also need to choose where and what you are going to trade. For shares, you need to decide whether you are going to trade in UK shares, US shares or in a different country entirely, although that is much harder than the two main English-speaking markets. In each market, there are several different exchanges: the London Stock Exchange and the AIM in the UK, Wall Street or the NASDAQ in the US, and so on. You need to choose an account that offers

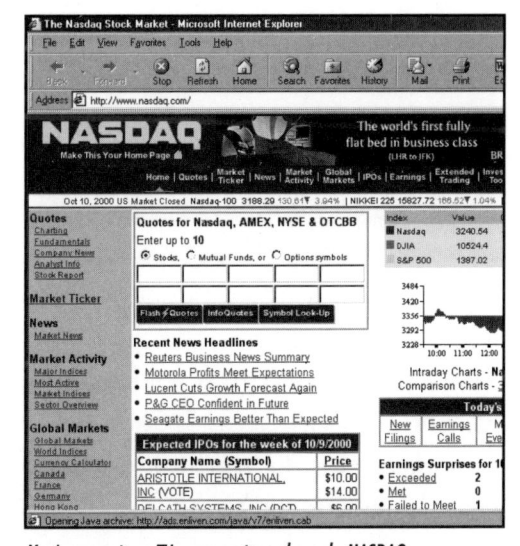

You've seen it on TV, now see it on the web: NASDAQ.

trading in your preferred market.

The other factor to consider is commission. Each broker will charge a different level of commission or fee for each transaction, often based on how frequently you intend to trade. On the share side of things there are numerous different options to choose from, so it pays to commit some time to serious research so as little as possible of your profits disappears into the commission the online brokers charge.

Once you have chosen a broker, you need to set up an account. This usually involves giving some proof of identity and then paying in a minimum sum to the trading account. Again, this may vary from broker to broker.

Now, you're ready to start playing the markets. The big question is where to invest your money. Making good trading decisions is based on solid research into what you are trading. Information about companies is more freely available than information relevant to futures or currency markets, which is one of the reasons shares are traded more extensively online.

One of your first ports of call should be companies' own web sites. Any public company has to provide detailed financial information to both current and future investors. Most companies now provide this on their web site, usually in an 'investor relations' section. Trading statements are posted for download to your own computer, where you can look at them on screen or print them out for future reference. These will include a summary of the audited accounts and statements of the company's direction, successes and failures by the main board directors.

Many sites also post regularly updated information about the way the company is trading, both to attract new investors and reassure the existing ones. Press releases about new projects, launches and deals are one way of doing this.

Beyond the information the company itself provides there are several other ways of gaining useful data. Some on-line news services provide both free and paid-for investor information. For example, Reuters offers both a basic, time-lagged share price and financial information service for free and a more extensive, detailed and up-to-date version for a fee.

The stock exchanges themselves usually include downloadable data on their web sites, which give you a good picture of the overall market climate.

However, this data is all fairly bland and on the whole relates to events which have already happened and therefore have already affected the share price. Furthermore, while past performance is one basis upon which you can make a decision, as the financial services adverts say, it is in no way a guarantee of future performance.

RISKY BUSINESS

If you are willing to take a risk – and if you aren't you really shouldn't be fooling around on the stock market – the best place to pick up gossip on the future of various companies is on an online discussion board dedicated to investing. There are a number of sites which stand out here: Raging Bull, Hemscott, Motley Fool and even the ubiquitous Yahoo!'s own site are worth a look.

Most of the discussions have at least a few knowledgeable, experienced dealers discussing particular companies or markets, so it's worth reading through the news items carefully for insights. Beware of trusting one person's information or insider tips too much, though. The boards are as open to clueless would-be experts, who are happy to express an opinion on something they know nothing about, as they are to people who really understand the markets.

Many of these sites also provide good, independent guides to the whole investing process, which are well worth a read.

Of course, TV, radio and the newspapers also all carry financial and stock market information and it pays to keep abreast of it if you plan on trading your shares regularly.

While on the issue of information and education, it's worth noting that many of the specialist online brokerages provide online education and advice packages on the whole trading process. The Charles Schwab site is particularly good in this regard and is well worth a visit, even if you choose to use another broker.

Once you have made your decision about a group of companies that seem worth investing in, it's time to start making your deals. Like the stock markets themselves, investing through the Internet is not a 24-hour business. Each exchange only opens for a limited period of time each day, and most don't trade on weekends. Therefore, any buy or sell orders you place through the web site of your chosen broker can only be processed if the exchange is actually open at that time. If not, you'll find your instructions will be queued until the exchange opens next. That's risky, as the biggest changes in share price often happen at the beginning of the trading day, as people try to do big purchases or off-load a lot of shares before other people notice and the share price changes.

So, you should try to make any changes to your investments while the market is open. Because the online brokers' systems can interface directly with the stock markets' main trading computers, most of the time your deals will happen virtually instantaneously.

However, stock prices change from second to second, so the price at the time your deal goes through might be different from the share price you saw when you started the transaction. Generally you will not be able to specify the exact amount you want for your shares, or that you are going to pay for new ones. Instead you will be restricted to slightly vaguer options like specifying a maximum price you are prepared to pay for a purchase or the

Etrade is undeniably popular – but is it effective?

minimum amount you will accept for a sale. The easiest option is to settle for the 'best available' option where the computer systems just gets the best deal it can when the transaction goes through.

TRADING SITES

http://www.barclays-stockbrokers.co.uk
This UK bank has recently moved into online stockbroking and is pushing the service heavily with TV advertising. A serious player but it will soon be joined by most of the other UK banks, with HSBC due to join the sector shortly.

http://www.etrade.co.uk/
A UK-orientated online service with some good additional information.

http://www.halifax.co.uk
The Halifax offers a quick and easy share-dealing service called ShareXpress for smaller investors.

http://www.schwab-worldwide.com/europe/
The mighty American online dealer also has a UK presence with some great tutorials and a range of various accounts.

http://www.selftrade.co.uk
This site aims to make trading as simple as possible, a philosophy that is reflected in its design.

INFORMATION SOURCES

http://www.fool.co.uk/
A wide-ranging site, covering all sorts of financial matters, but with good advice and a lively discussion board supporting the online share-dealer.

http://www.hemscott.net
A comprehensive and detailed site with a lot of in-depth information about different companies and services for the small investor.

http://www.ragingbull.altavista.com/
Targeted directly at the share investor and no-one else, Alta Vista's Raging Bull service has a lively discussion board.

http://uk.finance.yahoo.com/
A comprehensive site offering of all sorts of financial information from Yahoo! which provides plenty of material for company analysis.

ONLINE GAMBLING

Thanks to some sensationalist coverage as the media first became aware of the Internet, in many people's mind it is associated with vice. Sex was covered in gaudy detail with the scare stories about the availability of pornography. Drugs, too, became a source of concern with stories ranging from being able to order drugs online to dealers using the Internet to co-ordinate their activities.

As coverage of the Net became more sophisticated and people grew aware of the reality of the situation, stories like this faded away. In the meantime another vice, and a legal one, on the whole, has slowly built up an online following: gambling.

Now, gambling online is no surer a way of making money than it is in the real world. It's just that gambling online is faster and easier, and doesn't require you to dress up to go to a casino.

The appeal of setting up a casino online is the international nature of the Internet. For example, in the US, running a gambling business is illegal in the vast majority of the states. Nevada was the exception, and so the small town of Las Vegas turned into an internationally-renowned, glitzy city entirely based on gambling. Equally, run an online casino from a state where it's legal or from somewhere offshore, and suddenly you can take your business to the whole country.

Equally, the UK's laws on gambling may have liberalized a little in recent years, but getting a licence for a casino is a lengthy, complicated and expensive process. The cost of setting it up after you get the licence is another deterrent. All of these obstacles or costs are minimized by setting up an online gambling facility.

That's not to say that governments are entirely happy about this sort of thing. The US Congress is busily trying to pass some law that will outlaw online gambling within the United States. However, with online gambling revenues in the $1.2 billion range in 1999, it's a big business and not one that will be stamped out easily.

If you take a careful look at most of the web sites that offer online gaming, most have statements to the effect that all the bets are considered to be received in somewhere like Antigua. This is simply because Antigua is one of the few places worldwide that will issue operators with licences for online gambling.

That said, some of the UK's most respected players in the betting and gambling game are online and doing very nicely, thank you. Ladbrokes, William Hill and even the Tote are all represented in the virtual world.

Of course, these operations thrive because they are easy to use. Anyone with a credit card and Internet access can gamble from their security of their own home. The anonymity and ease of

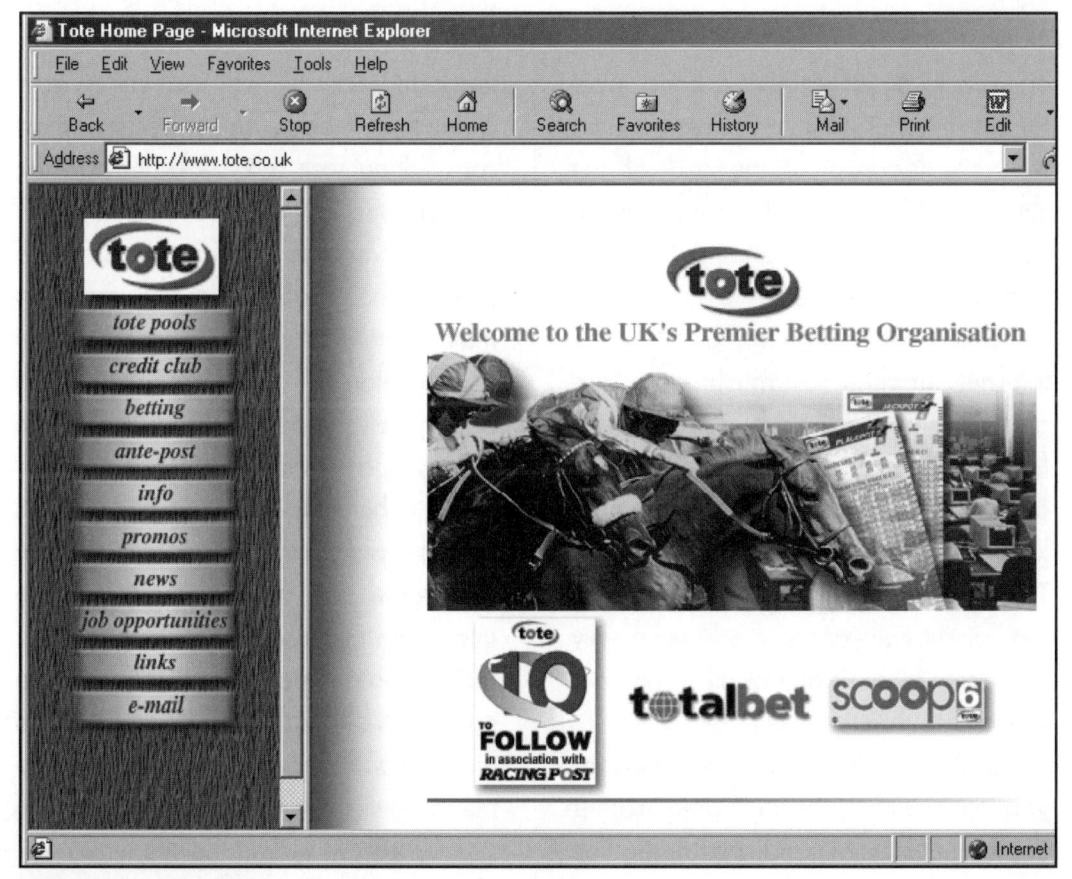

Tote is also present on the web.

the process appeals to many would-be gamblers.

If you want to join their ranks in the hope of making your fortune through the auspices of Lady Luck, there are some things you must bear in mind. The first, and most important, is to look very carefully at the site you choose. Gambling sites have been a rich vein for Internet fraudsters, and giving them your credit card details isn't the best way in the world of getting rich.

Stick to the sites of well-known existing operators, or alternatively head over to the Internet Gaming Commission's web site (address at the end of the chapter). This lists only licensed sites, so your financial details should be safer with sites you find there.

The site claims that more than 650 Internet gaming establishments are operating in more than 30 countries, from Antigua and Australia to Trinidad and Venezuela. Of these 650 gaming locations nearly 125 are not licensed. That means, of course, that they are not regulated by anyone and you have very little come-back, if any at all, if you are taken for a ride.

The Commission's site also cautions you to watch out for some rather unpleasant special conditions in the fine print such as 'winnings in excess of $2,000 may, at the discretion of the casino, be paid out in instalments not to exceed $2,000 per month'. That's a sure way to stop you getting your hands on any big winnings, and this is a book about making money on the web.

So, how do you choose a site? Most of them work in one of two ways. A few sites ask you to download software which connects to the Internet to do the gambling. On the whole, this software is only available for PCs, so users of Macs and other operating systems are out in the cold. Sites which use this system claim that it offers better security than conventional web browser-based betting.

Most sites just use the web browser, though. Everyone who has access to the Internet has one on their computer, making the market widely accessible.

Some sites only give you the option to bet against the dealer – in other words to play against the computer hosting the game. Other sites will let you play against other people, online. This appeals to a lot of people, as the degree of social interaction increases if the site has a chat facility. More importantly, the competitive edge between real people can drive bets higher than they would go if it was merely the computer you were facing.

Once you've picked the site, you need to set up an account before you can start playing. Some sites may have a minimum entry stake, so check before you commit yourself to a particular site. As with most sites where money is being transferred, you will be asked to register, create an account and provide credit card details.

You can then use your credit card to buy 'chips' or some other form of virtual token which you use to make your bets, just like in a real casino. Not surprisingly, most of the web sites go out of their way to make the experience feel as much like real casinos as possible. After all, the ambience is part of what you buy into when you gamble in this way.

If the site is hosted abroad, as most are, and is run in a currency other than your own, check the currency conversion rates the site is offering when you purchase chips and make sure they are broadly in line with actual bank exchange rates. Otherwise you may find yourself down before you even start playing.

Once those details are set up, you are ready to start placing your bets. Next, you have to pick a game. There will probably be a wide variety on offer. Here's a selection of the most common ones:

Blackjack, otherwise known as pontoon or twenty-one, is a very simple game. The players are each dealt two cards with the goal of reaching a total combined value of all their cards of 21 without going over. The player may draw as many cards as he wants until reaching 21. If the player draws a card that puts him over 21 he is said to be 'bust', and he loses the hand. A winning hand adds up to the closest to 21 without busting.

Roulette is a casino classic, often seen in the movies. The player places a bet on a number, colour, or group of numbers on the roulette table. The roulette wheel is spun, and a small ball dropped into it. The winnings are determined by where the ball lands. Of course, online there is no real wheel or ball, so a random computer program generates the result.

Generally, a roulette table is marked with the numbers 0 to 36. The numbers are alternately coloured red and black with 0 coloured green. You bet by placing tokens on areas on the virtual table representing numbers, colours or a particular group of numbers like odds or evens. The winnings (if any) are determined based on the particular area of the table you won with. Each has different odds.

Some sites emulate fruit machines (also known as slot machines or one-armed bandits). If you've spent any time in a gaming hall, you'll know how these work. You drop in a small amount of money, and the pictures in three small windows spin. If they settle into one of the winning patterns, you get the cash. If they don't, you lose. Occasionally, the machine will give you the option to 'hold', which allows you to re-spin, while holding on to some of the old pictures, or 'nudge' which allows you to move a picture wheel one picture round in the hope of getting a winning combination.

Other games from poker to baccarat are available, but explaining them and how they work is well beyond the scope of this book. If you want to learn them, buy a book and practise with other people for no money before you try playing online.

In fact, most card or casino games are available somewhere on the Internet, so if you have a favourite game, chances are you can play it online if you wish.

Online betting isn't limited to casino-style games, though. If it's a rainy day, and you don't fancy a trip down to the local bookmaker, you can bet on races, sports events, elections and any other event that catches your eye online too. As mentioned earlier, most of the traditional British bookmakers can be found online.

The service they offer is generally not much more than a web-enabled version of the telephone betting services they have been offering for years. You place a bet on a particular event happening. You are given odds when you place the bet of that event occurring. If it happens, say a particular horse comes first or your chosen single hits the top spot at Christmas, you get winnings based on the bet you placed and the odds you got when you placed the bet.

Minimum bets vary from a few pennies to a few pounds, but once you have registered with the site they can be placed quickly and easily online, wherever you are. Results can be sent to you via emails or, in the case of some sites, via WAP or SMS phones. It's a long way from pencil stubs and betting slips in a smoke-filled booky's.

These services also make it easier for you to find unusual bets to risk your cash on. The William Hill site does a nice line in American sporting and political bets, which might take your fancy, especially if you are from the US and find yourself unable to bet on your own sports.

Thanks to the National Lottery, lotteries have become something of a national obsession over the last few years in the UK. While you can't play the National Lottery online yet, a few on-line lottery sites have sprung up. Some are simple lotteries, based on picking a certain set of numbers. Other are more quirky, including one based on football results, not unlike the football pools.

One unusual lottery site is Bananalotto. It is different from most other lottery sites in that it doesn't cost you a penny to place a bet. Instead, the site forces you to follow a link to an advertiser's web site, before it registers your bet. For the chance to win something for nothing, a few seconds glancing at an advertiser's web site is a small price to play, or so runs the theory.

CASINOS
http://www.internetcommission.com
The site that keeps an eye on which on-line casinos are licensed and which aren't. It offers loads of advice on the problems and potential pitfalls in the world of internet gaming, too, so is well worth a look.

BOOKMAKERS
http://www.tote.co.uk
The Tote, a familiar site at most race courses and dog tracks, around the UK at least, is also open for cyber-betting and has the facility to set up a simple credit account.

http://www.willhill.co.uk
The self-proclaimed 'most respected name in British bookmaking' offers bets on events both at home and abroad in a multitude of languages. Based in Antigua – so you'll rather pleasantly find that there is no tax on winnings.

Betting sites are increasingly common in the UK.

http://www.bet.co.uk
Behind the short and to the point web address lives the site of high street bookmaker Ladbrokes, offering the normal betting services.

OTHERS
http://www.bananalotto.co.uk
The free lottery, based on enforced viewing of advertisers' web sites.

http://www.lotter-e.co.uk
A lottery based on Premier League football results.

BUYING AND SELLING YOUR HOME

In many people's eyes the one great thing the Internet could do for them and others would be to clear the estate agent out of the property-buying process. While many property dealers are professionals, there are enough unscrupulous companies out there to make life for the house seller very, very hard work.

A few years back, an answer started to appear. A handful of web sites sprang up offering to let you market your home online. In essence, they were not very different from the small ads section of your local newspaper in that all they did was allow you to publicise the fact that you had a property for sale and then give some basic information. Of course, the advantage of the Internet was that it allowed you to reach a far greater audience at a cost that was little different from what you'd pay for that newspaper ad.

People have picked up the Internet house-hunting habit quickly. It's no surprise: it is much, much easier to sit at home doing searches on several web sites than it is to trek your way round ten estate agents explaining to each what are you are looking for, and making sure you see all suitable properties. Such sites also offer many more services than most conventional estate agents. They will update you on the status of properties you are interested in through SMS messages on your mobile phone or email. You can store details of properties you are interested in online, or email them to your partner.

For the truly lazy house-hunter, you can register your requirements and be emailed whenever something suitable hits the market. The sites also offer help in other aspects of the moving process. For example one major site, assertahome.co.uk, offers more than 1,700 mortgage products from more than 50 providers. Most of the big sites are stuffed full of advice on the house-moving process.

So things have moved on a little since the early days. First of all, the insurance and mortgage companies steamed into the marketplace, offering their own online estate agencies as well as online deals for acquiring mortgages, house insurance and other services invaluable to the homeowner.

The estate agents didn't like this one little bit, seeing it as a direct threat to their own business, and so they started to make their own presence felt. Initially, they signed deals with some of the existing online sites and handed over their property listings for posting on the Internet. In the last few months a new development has come to light. Many of

Some sites offer all you need for buying and selling a home, including mortgage advice.

the top estate agents are starting to band together to launch their own site. The organization is currently known as Fastcrop, though that will change before the site itself launches.

The reasoning behind these moves is that it is the listings of available homes that make these site work. Buyers come to them because they have good, comprehensive lists of properties available in all the areas they are searching for the perfect home.

How does this affect you, the would-be seller? Obviously, you will want to tap into the marketing power of the Net. You might even want to use it to try and reduce your costs. However, you have a number of options from which you need to pick carefully.

The first thing that you need to be aware of is that, for the foreseeable future, you can't actually sell a house fully online. The existing legislation that governs house sales (in the UK at least – check your own country) is worded in such a way that it forces all property transactions to at some point involve written contracts which are physically signed. A digital signature doesn't cut it in legislation written decades before people had working computers. While the Land Registry is working to change this, it will be several years before those efforts come to fruition.

However, you can use the Internet to speed up parts of the process. You have two options. The first is to do it yourself. The key to this is to use one of the few web sites that allow private property owners to place their own houses on them. Have a look at the sites that are out there: they have a range of different presentation styles and charges for their services, so it pays to shop around. Most sites will ask you to contact them directly and will talk you through the steps involved in selling your house yourself.

Once your site is chosen, the first thing you have to do is to measure the whole of the house as accurately as you possibly can. You also need to have good photographs taken, and scanned well, if the site you choose doesn't do this itself. Online property details, on the whole, are much like printed details. You have the physical sizes of the properties. You have the photograph. You have contact details. Everything else is up to you.

If you are going it alone, you now have a whole host of issues to consider. To establish the value of your property, look at similar homes in your area and base your asking price on that. You could, of course, ask several estate agents for valuations in order to establish the market price, but you will almost certainly have to pay for this if you are not using them to market your property.

You'll need to set aside a marketing budget. Internet sites do charge for putting your details up. You might want to put up a sale board to catch passing buyers. You will need to check with the planning department of your local authority before you put up that For Sale sign at last.

It might be worth investing in some flashy online photography. Sites like ehouse and iPIX offer virtual reality images of rooms which you can email to interested parties, or put on the site, if your chosen site supports this. The price starts at around £100. For this a photographer will come to the house and photograph particular rooms repeatedly.

The images are then stitched together digitally and assembled into a continuous 360-degree image which can be rotated with your mouse.

Without an agent to represent you, you'll need to be available to potential buyers as much as possible. An email address on your advertising certainly helps, but at the very least a mobile phone and a good answering machine at home are going to make a world of difference.

You will also have to do all the house viewings yourself. Allow viewers to walk around freely, and be ready to answer questions. Most of all, do not let any criticism they make get to you. Yes, it's your home, but feeling insulted because of something they have said is not going to smooth the sale process.

Having your own structural survey may help the sale move forward faster. The Royal Institution of Chartered Surveyors' web site can help you track down a local firm who can do the survey.

You can do your own conveyancing – the legal process of transferring the ownership of a property from one person to another – if you want. However, it is a very risky business. There are several legal obligations to be met, to do with informing different parties of what the sale involves, the sale price and so on.

Also, if you do not use a solicitor, you have to do many of the most important pre-contract stages yourself. For example, as a buyer, you have to do a search on the property in the local authority's files, to check there is nothing planned for the area that will affect future ownership. As a seller, if you mess up the legal side of the sale, you open yourself to legal action by the buyer if everything wasn't done according to the guidelines laid down in law.

That's not to say that you can't do it,

if you want. Just ask yourself carefully if the risk and the time and effort involved are worth the financial saving. If you decide they're not, ask your bank or building society to recommend a licensed conveyancer or solicitor. It is often best to ask a local firm as they will be more familiar with the area, but get a written quotation before asking them to start work. It is also worth checking whether they subscribe to Land Registry Direct. This is an online service which allows searches to be done in a fraction of the time they normally are. However, it cannot be accessed by the general public.

The other option, of course, is to sign up with an estate agent who has a strong Internet presence. You have two choices. You can either sign up with an agent who has a strong web site for the company, or you can sign up with an agent through one of the national web sites.

To find a local firm with a good site requires the same effort as finding any good local agent: wandering high streets and talking to the companies themselves. Be sure to have a good look at their web sites and check how easily findable they are on search engines before you commit to one firm. Don't forget to compare prices, either, and see if they charge extra for Internet advertising.

The other option is to find a national web site you like, and find a local agent through them. A list of some of the better-known sites is available at the end of this chapter, but an Internet index like Yahoo! will list many more.

Once again the style of the sites varies wildly. Some, like fish4homes, are clearly targeted at the younger and funkier end of the market. Others are more corporate and bland, suiting all types of house sale. Look for a combination of a design that you think will attract the sort of buyer that suits your neighbourhood and prices for the web marketing services to guide your decision.

The national sites will let you search their list of affiliated agents to find one who is based nearby. Not all sites have good coverage of all regions of the country, so if you don't find a nearby agent, it's well worth trying a different site. Don't forget to check the additional charges an estate agent is looking for to sell your property: that will normally involve a percentage commission and that varies from site to site.

If all this seems like too much work, there's one final option. Most of the sites will allow you to register your house for potential tenants. Forgetting the whole sale process and becoming a landlord instead is another way to make money out of the web.

SOME TOP SITES
http://www.assertahome.co.uk
One of the major players in the on-line sales market. The site is backed by financial services company CGNU.

http://www.fastcrop.com
Several hundred estate agents have banded together to form this site which will start trading in 2001.

http://www.fish4homes.co.uk
Another national site, backed by a consortium of newspaper owners. Just one of a whole range of fish4… sites, most of which are dedicated to Internet buying.

http://www.rightmove.co.uk
Another site backed by financial services companies, this time Countrywide Assured and Royal & SunAlliance.

http://www.08004homes.com
Formerly known as home2home.co.uk, this site offers a range of additional information and a seller's guide.

http://www.homedirectory.com
This site offers iPIX 360-degree photography, an American competitor to ehouse (below), as part of its marketing package.

http://www.itlhomes.co.uk
One of the original independent sites, and one of the few that will accept properties from individual sellers.

http://www.connells.co.uk
An example of an individual firm that posts properties to its web site. Connell is affiliated to rightmove.co.uk, one of the national players.

OTHER RELATED SITES
http://www.ehouse.co.uk
A site which offers virtual reality house pictures to help market your property.

http://www.hometrack.co.uk
Provides statistics about the housing market in your local area. Invaluable if you are going it alone.

http://www.rics.org
Homepage of the Royal Institution of Chartered Surveyors, which allows you to search for surveyors working in your area.

http://www.titleabsolute.com
A firm which offers conveyancing services online.

SHOPPING

Not long after the World Wide Web really got going, it got popular. It was originally a massive source of information but it didn't take long at all for it to become what many investors and financial forecasters hoped it would be: a huge marketplace. Now on the Internet you can buy whatever you want whenever you want.

If all else fails, one of the best ways to keep feeling wealthy is to spend as little as possible on what you buy. At first glance the Internet appears ideal for this. From the very early days of consumer awareness of the Net, its shopping sites have been associated with discounts. Amazon made much of its book discounts when it launched, for example.

Let's face it, though, web shopping has taken a bit of a hammering. The failure of e-commerce sites like boo.com, which sold fashion sportswear, and clickmango.com, a health and beauty retailer that was backed by TV star Joanna Lumley, has led many people to think that Internet shopping was failing.

They're wrong. There are numerous online retailers out there still. Amazon, once merely an online bookseller, has expanded to become a veritable online shopping mall. Now it offers everything from software to music to books, along with all sorts of other goods through partner web sites. It has stuck to its guns, and continues to offer spectacular discounts on a large proportion of its stock, although these are sometimes outweighed by the postage charges for having the goods delivered to your home.

Sites like bol.com are diversifying, too. In fact, if you look long and hard enough, there are online shops selling most types of goods. However, many of them have very uncertain backing at the moment, and many more online shops may follow boo.com down the virtual toilet pan.

Finding online retailers isn't hard. Despite the funding problems that have beset the dotcom retailers, all those bus-sides, advertising hoardings and TV breaks are still full of advertisements for new online retailers.

However, if you are looking for something in particular, search engines are the way to go. In particular those web sites like yahoo.co.uk, which offer an index of particular web sites, are very useful. Doing a search on 'retailers' and the particular type of goods you're interested in will usually bring up a list of shops selling what you want in a particular category.

However, you might find that many of the names you see listed are very familiar. High street retailers, rather than seeing the Internet as a threat (as it was originally touted) have started to see it as an opportunity. Even that most traditional of retailers, Marks & Spencer, now has an online store, offering a selection of both its clothing and other goods sold in its stores.

This online presence isn't restricted to the big chains, either. Department stores like Debenhams can be found online, too, as can one-off shops. Most of these retailers have extravagant sites that showcase their latest range of goods. Many sites stop there: they provide online catalogues and marketing but nothing else. However, increasing numbers are providing secure online shopping as well.

The process of shopping online is pretty much the same whether you are using the Internet version of a high-street retailer or an online-only dotcom shop. You browse through the site selecting the goods you want to buy. When you choose something you want, you click on a button on-screen that adds it to your virtual shopping basket. In effect all that happens is that the computer running the web site remembers that you've asked for that particular item.

When you have had enough shopping, you click on the 'checkout' button. You will be asked to register, giving a user name and password and, if this is the first time you have shopped with this particular online site, your name, address, contact details and a payment method – usually a credit or even debit card. Some sites will store the payment card details for you, speeding up future purchases. However, because of worries expressed in the press about the security of credit card information during online purchases, other retailers have chosen not to retain this information to reassure their customers, and to minimize the risk of fraud if someone manages to guess your user name and password.

You will then be presented with a page summarizing your purchases. You are given a last opportunity to change your mind about some or all of them. When you have confirmed what you want, the computer will calculate the total cost, including all taxes and postage, and ask your approval to proceed with the purchase. You may be offered a range of different postage options. Examine these carefully: in most circumstances standard parcel post of your national mail delivery is fine. However, if the goods are valuable, you might want to think about choosing a more expensive option with more safeguards.

If you press 'yes' the computer will normally pause for a while, while the site gets approval for your credit card. Once it is approved, you'll get a screen confirming that your order has been processed. You will normally be sent an email confirmation, too.

Many conventional retailers who also have catalogues allow you to use the two in tandem. You type in the number of the item you want from the catalogue into the web site, and immediately it brings it up, without your having to click your way through the site to find it.

There are problems, though. Most of the time, shopping from the web branch of a conventional retailer will actually cost you more than if you went into one of that chain's shops. As well as paying the same price for your goods as you would in stores, you end up paying for packaging and delivery as well. Tesco.com, for example, adds £5 to the cost of your shopping to pay for its next-day delivery by van.

To offset this, and to try and attract more customers to their Web stores, most retailers run Internet-exclusive sales and promotions of various sorts through the year. So it pays to keep checking back to your favourite Web sites to see if there are any deals going. Some sites allow you to subscribe to an email newsletter which will inform you of any new bargains or sales as they go live on the Web site. Of course, some retailers do offer cheaper prices on their web sites, but they are in a minority.

Some goods are easier to buy over the net than others. Books, CDs, videos and computer games have all proved sure fire hits. Computer hardware and other electrical goods have also proved surprisingly successful. Clothes have been problematic, though.

The problem with the clothing retailers' web sites is twofold. As with catalogue shopping, you can't actually try the goods on. No matter how good the item looks on the model in the beautifully composed picture on the screen, if it doesn't fit you when it arrives, it has to

You can buy a lot more than just ordinary supermarket food at Tesco.com.

go back. Boo.com's attempt to provide virtual dummies on which you could try the clothes for fit was an expensive technical nightmare, and one of the problems behind its failure. So, until a better idea comes along, you're stuck with pictures of models whose proportions are, sadly, unlikely to match your own.

Those pictures are the second problem. By its very nature, clothes shopping is a visual pursuit, and that means pictures. Unless you have a very fast Internet connection, online clothes shopping can be a time-consuming business, while you wait for the pictures to crawl their way to your computer. Using catalogues alongside web sites as described above is one answer to this, but that's not truly online retailing.

However, other sectors of the market have responded to the threat of the

Internet retailers in kind. Both book and CD retailers, like Borders and HMV, now have web sites with search facilities and online ordering. Books and CDs are better suited to online shopping, because their descriptions can be text-based and the images need not be large. Both sectors have a significant advantage over their bricks-and-mortar cousins: they can carry a huge range of albums or books that it just wouldn't be economic for a high-street shop to stock. If you're hunting for obscure albums by barely known bands or early novels by minor authors, the Internet can save you a lot of time and money in searching out exactly what you require.

One sector that has had particular success with the Internet is supermarkets. Tesco in particular has tapped a niche by discovering that many people will be happy to pay that extra few pounds on

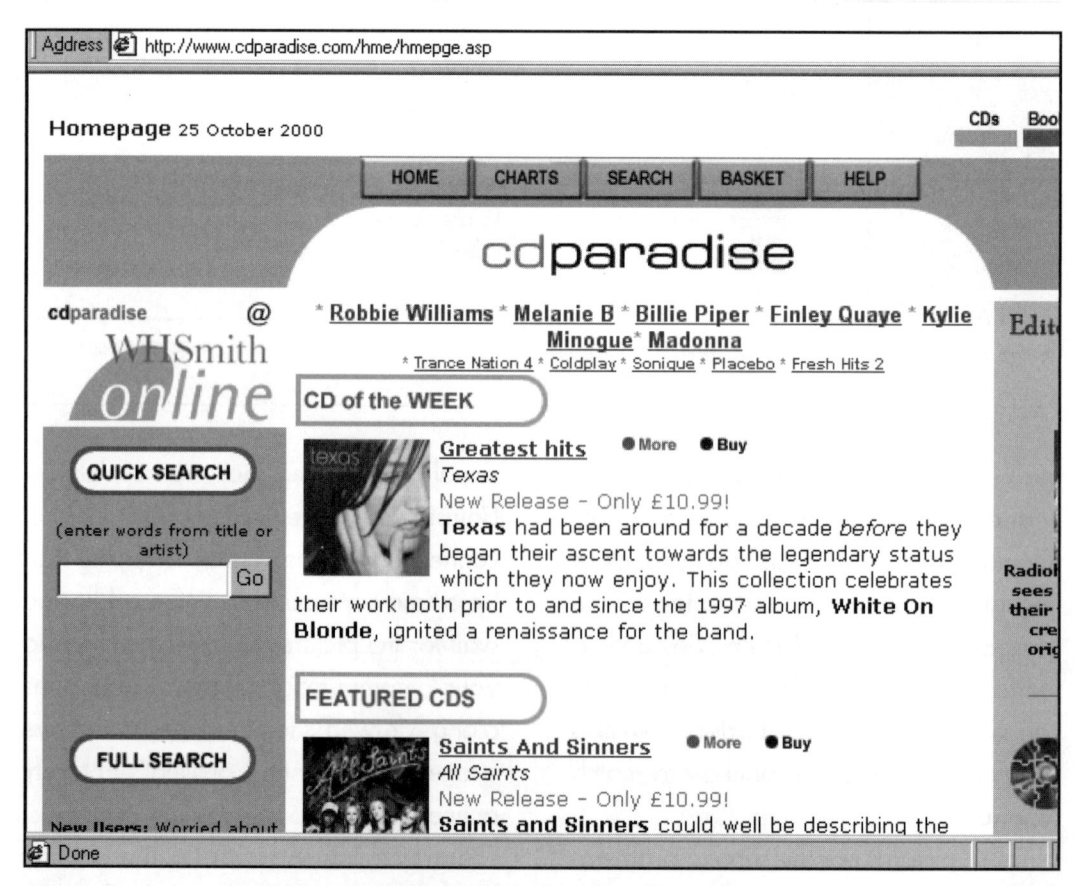

CDs are among the most-purchased goods on the Internet. There are hundreds of companies selling.

their shopping bill if they can have the goods delivered to their home. Users of the Tesco Direct service can do all their shopping via the Tesco web site, provided they have a store that offers the service nearby, and have it delivered during a time slot of their choosing. Shopping for groceries online is initially a time-consuming process as you have to select every item individually, often on different screens. Luckily, once you have a 'regular order' of the basic goods you buy on most visits, it is much quicker to add the extra items on each visit. There's also the complication of not being able to assess the quality of your fruit or meat before you buy, so many people omit fresh foods from their Internet shopping session.

Finding the online version of your favourite retailers is a lot easier than tracking down an Internet-only retailer. The first and most obvious route is to look at the shop's own promotional material. Shopping bags, catalogues, TV and print adverts all carry the URLs of shops' web sites. Sometimes the window of their shops do too. However, if that doesn't work, you can always just try typing the name of the shop into your browser's address window with '.co.uk' or '.com' after it. One of those two, or possibly both, should bring up the web site.

Alternatively you can try a more traditional route and just do a search for the shop's name on a search engine or web index. Most will be registered so long as they haven't opened their virtual shopfront too recently.

A last option is to look at the web site of your local shopping centre or mall. From Bluewater, one of the big centres, in Kent, (www.bluewater.co.uk), to Lewisham Shopping Centre in south-east London (www.lewishamcentre.co.uk), many shopping centres now have a web presence. Some of them contain links to retailers' own web sites.

Here's a few to get you started:
http://www.hmv.co.uk
http://www.next.co.uk
http://www.marksandspencer.com
http://www.principles.co.uk
http://www.waterstones.co.uk
http://www.tesco.com
http://www.debenhams.com

However, why buy new? Second-hand and swapped goods can be a very good way of obtaining what you need as cheaply as possible. The web has allowed second-hand dealers of all sorts to reach a dramatically wider audience. The concept is very basic. The dealers acquire second-hand goods from a whole range of sources, and offer them for sale through the web site. Admittedly, not all of the more specialist sites have a full e-commerce facility. Many just advertise the service and the availability of products, and then expect you to phone or visit their shop. This isn't always a bad thing: who would want to buy a second-hand agricultural grain drier without having the chance to physically inspect it first?

Still, they provide a viable alternative to paying the full price for goods. Many of the technology or machinery-related sites maintain and repair their goods before selling, and provide good guarantees on the products. Getting hold of goods like CDs and books is a little more reliable than it is through auction sites. Many web sites will allow you to register a wants list and will email you if they find what you are looking for at a future point.

Providing a comprehensive listing of these sites would be nigh on impossible and fairly pointless as many of them tackle extremely specialist markets. For a complete list, try searching for 'second hand' on a Web index like Yahoo!

Here are a few examples:

http://www.laptopshop.co.uk – specialises in second-hand laptop computers and spare components

http://www.masterfarm.co.uk – specialises in second-hand grain driers

http://www.dustycovers.com – a second-hand bookshop

http://www.uksportscars.com – sells classic British cars

Another option for getting hold of goods cheaply is exchange sites. These work on a basic 'swap shop' principle, reminiscent of the old Saturday morning kids' show of the same name from the 80s. Like auction sites (Chapter 17) these sites allow you to dispose of unwanted goods. Rather than selling them for money, though, you can list something you want in exchange and hopefully find someone willing to make that swap.

For example, if you had an unwanted set of spanners, and wanted any Corrs CD, you would register with the site and post 'Set of Spanners' as what you had and 'Corrs CD' as what you wanted. You would then wait until someone with a Corrs CD, or something they thought is similar enough, made an offer through the site. Obviously you could accept or reject this as you saw fit.

Some sites also give you the option to just sell the unwanted goods for a set price. While this doesn't offer the same opportunity to maximize the price you get for them as in an auction, it's easier (fewer limits on how long your goods can be on offer for, for example). Auctions are limited in time, you have to pay to have the auction restarted if you failed to sell in this time.

Once you decide to accept an offer, you have to exchange the goods. Both parties normally pay for their own shipping, and most sites specify the goods must be posted within three days of the sale finishing. Some sites offer special shipping services to facilitate the process. The same risks apply as with any goods exchange organised through the Internet. For more details of the problems or precautions to take, see Chapter 17.

If you go for the sale option, some sites take payment for you, releasing it to you only when the goods arrive. A few offer a form of insurance, in case you are cheated by unscrupulous buyers.

Here are a few exchange sites:
http://www.ukgamesexchange.co.uk –
    a used computer game swap site
http://www.swapwell.com –
    offers 'garage sales' of second-hand goods as well as swap or buy options on unwanted goods
http://www.webswappers.com –
    a fast and bright-looking swap site

One quirky example of this kind of site is called Swapitshop.com. This site offers kids the chance to swap old, unwanted toys online. Children, with permission from their parents or guardians, can register with the site for free. They then start accumulating 'Swappits', either through putting goods up to be swapped, or through various promotions run in the real world.

The accumulated Swappits can be used to bid for items others have put up for swapping. The site looks pretty good, and to the eternal relief of parents there isn't a single credit card involved in the process.

There are some absolute bargains to be found on the Net in other ways. Some come from specialist sites that have been set up to sell off retailers' unwanted goods which are no longer at their forefront of their range. This can range from electrical goods which have been supplanted by a better model, to clothes collections which have reached the end of their season.

However, by far the most common variation on this kind of site is the last-minute holiday retailer. These are a more sophisticated version of the bucket shops which try to sell off unsold seats cheap on behalf of airlines. The most famous online firm, by far, is lastminute.com.

The idea of these sites is to take unsold tickets for leisure activities of any sort and offer them to the public through a central, easily accessible source. The range of goods starts with flights and holidays and moves through to unusual days out, tables at restaurants, theatre tickets and even special goods. Bits left over from the demolition of Wembley Stadium were sold through lastminute.com!

The companies running the events benefit, because they sell tickets that would otherwise go to waste, the web site benefits because it takes a cut of the deal, and the customer benefits, because they get a cheap deal. It's also a great service if you are pathologically disorganized and never get round to booking holidays, arranging dates or buying presents early.

To take advantage of the deals these sites offer, you have to be flexible. Your

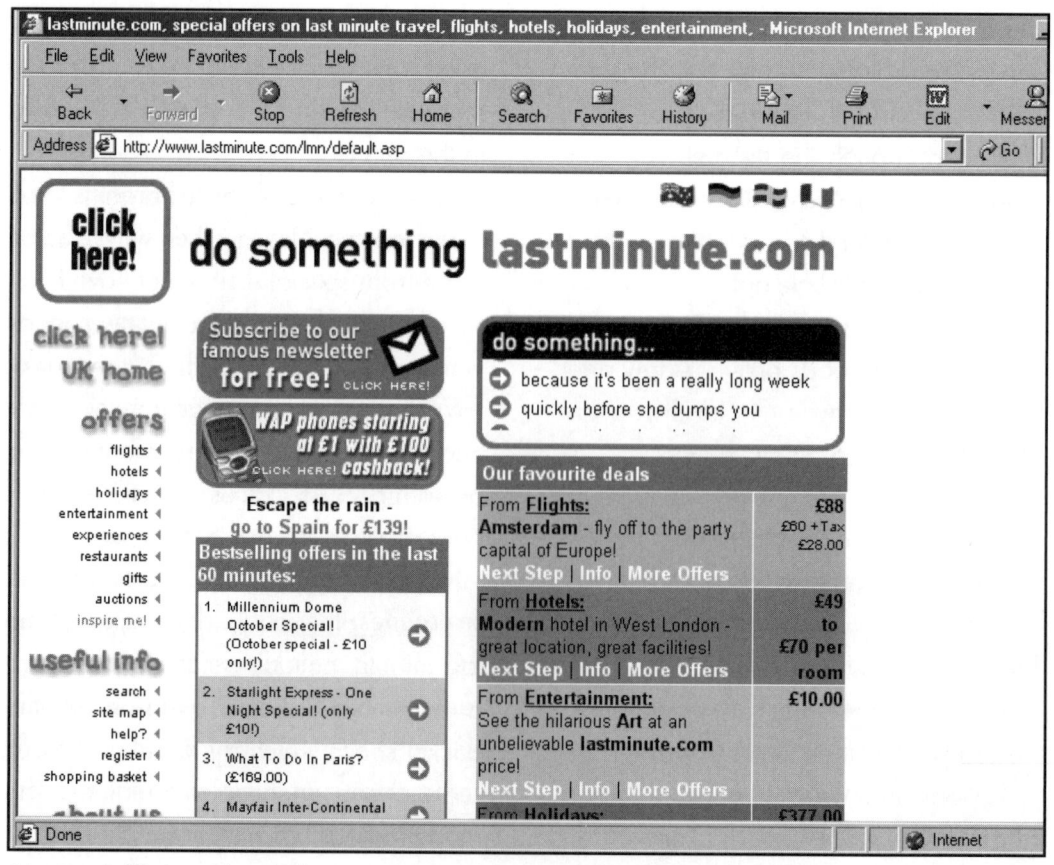

It is extremely difficult not to be tempted...

time, location, even type of holiday can be entirely dependent on what's on the site when you want to book. If you go with a set idea of what you want, the chances are you won't find it. It's possible that you won't find anything at all you would be happy to go on. Still, chances are you'll walk away with a decent discount, even if it's not an absolutely ideal holiday, event or present.

Some players in the last-minute holiday field:
http://www.bargainholidays.com
http://www.directholidays.co.uk
http://www.farebase.net
http://www.lastminute.com
http://www.latebreaks.com

Another way of saving money using the Web is to buy in bulk. Not on your own, mind, but in concert with others. Certain sites have been designed to harness the reach of the Internet to allow as many people as possible to benefit from the discounts you can get when you buy in bulk. If a business needs to buy tens or even hundreds of the same item, it is very easy for them to negotiate a bulk discount with the supplier. The individual, who is only buying one item – let's say a camera – can't hope to do the same thing. At best he might be able to find a couple of friends who also want to buy a camera, but that is probably not going to be sufficient to get a discount out of any retailer or manufacturer.

That's where bulk buying sites like letsbuyit.com come into their own. They allow people all over the country to buy things as a collective, thereby securing a discount. If our would-be camera buyer above went to one of these sites, and there was a camera he wanted on the site as one of the on-going sales, he could register to buy it. He would have to give the normal contact details and also a means of payment, which usually means a credit or debit card number. He also gets to specify a maximum price he is willing to pay.

The price of the camera starts at its normal retail price or thereabouts. As more people sign up to buy it, the price starts to drop. Like auctions (Chapter 17) the sale runs for a fixed period of time. When that is up, the number of people who have signed up to buy the camera determines the final, discounted price they pay. The maximum price mentioned earlier allows a would-be buyer to step out of the sale if the item's price stays out of his price range, because not enough people signed up.

If the target price has been reached or

better, though, his credit or debit card is charged for the goods and they are dispatched to him. This sort of buying power could not be assembled without the Internet. No other medium allows so many people in disparate locations to participate quickly and easily in the same sale, getting together to use their collective buying power as a bargaining tool.

Variations of this sort of site exist for small businesses as well. These sites allow firms to club together to buy stationery and office equipment at prices not dissimilar to what the really big companies can wring out of their suppliers. For a small business, anyhing that allows you compete with larger companies on a more equal footing is a boon, isn't it?.

The biggest single problem with shopping on the Internet is the so-called last mile – actually getting the goods delivered to you. While using a shopping site is usually fairly quick and easy, you then have to wait two or three days, and sometimes more, for your goods to arrive. A few sites have been set up in major cities, like UrbanFetch, with the intention of delivering to your door within hours of ordering, not days. However, this service is restricted to a limited range of goods and only a few of the bigger cities in the UK.

The other stumbling block is actually being there when the goods are delivered. Only a small proportion of what you can buy on the Net will actually fit through your letterbox. As most delivery companies do their rounds during the day, chances are that you'll be out when they try and drop off the parcel.

Getting your purchase sent to work instead might seem like an easy solution, but there are several problems with that. In many offices, most things that come through the door are opened centrally and then delivered to the individual they were addressed to. Your don't always want all your colleagues knowing what you are buying. Secondly, many companies will refuse to ship goods to any other address than the one your credit card is registered to – usually your home address. This is for both your and their protection. It makes it much harder for anyone who has got hold of your credit card number to rack up big online shopping bills using your account. It also, of course, makes it a lot harder for unscrupulous people to cheat the online retailers out of their goods.

At the time of writing, no easy way has been found around this problem. Lots of ideas have been suggested, from building secure drop-off storage points into people's houses to collection points in garages, supermarkets and local shops. However, these ideas are only in their infancy and it will be several years before they have a real impact on the e-shopping process.

In the meantime, some of the parcel courier services have started offering guaranteed evening delivery. This sounds like a good plan – you can make sure you're in and you have the rest of the evening to play with your new purchase. The drawback, though, is that they charge extra for the service. These additional costs, on top of the postage charges you are already paying to have your goods delivered, can very quickly turn a bargain into a very ordinary-priced product.

There is one product area that has found its way around this problem, though: software. More and more software companies are making their products not only available for online purchase, but also downloadable to your hard disk. This cuts out the need for the expensive packaging most applications and games come in, as well as the distribution process. Most manufacturers pass on a proportion of these savings to the customer, allowing you to get your hands on software much more cheaply than you could through specialist computer stores or even more conventional shops.

Some of the online retailers have jumped on the bandwagon – jungle.com offers a download shop, for instance. You are advised to back up the installer package you receive on to something like a Zip disk, or a CD if you have CD writer. If the worst comes to the worst and your hard drive corrupts completely without you having a back-up of the program, most shops will allow you to download it again at no extra cost, if you can prove you bought it. Keep a print-out of the email receipt you get somewhere safe, just in case.

Where this system falls down is if you have a slow Internet connection. If you have one of the high-speed ASDL, 'always on' services being rolled out by many of the larger Internet service providers, you will be OK. Applications of any size can be downloaded quickly and easily. However, if you only have a modem, you are going to be restricted to downloads of no more than 10 to 15 megabytes before your phone bill cancels out any savings you have made.

As (legally) downloadable music in compressed formats become more widely available, and e-books take off, a few of those delivery nightmares will be eased.

INDEX

08004homes 175
administration 41
adult site 10
advertising 60
advertising domains 125
advertising sites 24
afternic.com 37, 124
Alladvantage 111
Allcommunity 112
alluring domain names 36
Alta Vista rewards 110
Amazon.co.uk 31
Amazon.com 8
animations 16
Antigua offshore gambling 165
arcade games 12
assertahome 171
auction2.net 123
auctions 143
auctions abroad 151
Audience review sales sites 31
authors 46
available domains 118
Babylon X 10
Bananalotto 169
banking abroad 133
banks online 129
banner hits 26
Banner sites 24

banners 57, 71
Barclays 130
bargainholidays.com 185
Battle Net 13
Beenz 111
bidding process 145
bill payment companies 133
Books online 180
branded merchandise 109
break-even 40
Brochure sales sites 30
brokers 98, 160
bulk buying 185
bulk email 73
business documents 106
business overview 105
business plan 38
buying a house 170
buying at auction 144
buying goods online 177
buying shares 156
career opportunities 107
careful auction buying 148
casino sites 167
catalogues 105
CBS Appointments 137
CDs online 180
celebrities 10
certificate of registration 100

INDEX

checking domain availability 118
click-thru 24
collectibles 152
commission 160
contact addresses 67
conveyancing 173
cookies 54, 56, 80
corporate communications 106
counters 85
credit cards 43, 63
currency trading 157
customer databases 79
customer research 38, 42
Customer service 62
database sales 81
databases 79
Dave's Classics 12
DDM Direct 32
debenhams.com 181
delivering goods 186
department stores 177
digicash 129
Dilbert 12
domain auctions 122
domain charges 121
domain names 34, 116
domain registration 34
dotcom startups 7
doubleclick.com 72
download resource sites 26
download speed 52
downloadable sales 187
ebanking 128

ebusiness packages 50
ecash 128
ecommerce worth 6
ehouse 175
email lists 74
email marketing 73
enhancing business 104
enquiries 66
entertainment resource sites 28
estate agents 172, 174
etrade 163
exchange sites 182
expanding your site 88
feedback 67
finance 41
financial projections 38
finding jobs 138
foreign auctions 151
franchising 90
free web space 43
Freeserve 9
funding 38
gambling online 164
Gaming Commission 166
generic domains 126
geocities 44
getting rich 103
good CVs 139
goods exchanges 145
Guerrilla marketing 77
harvesting 80
high street stores 177
hit counters 56

INDEX

hit logs 96
home pages 21
house-hunting 170
how to gamble online 167
HSBC 131
HTML 47
IMDB 9
import restrictions 150
impression 72
Inbox Dollars 112
Information resource sites 26
internet auctions 144
internet banks 128
internet special offers 178
internetnews.com 86
interNIC 119
intrusiveness 53
investment banking 102
investor relations 106
IPO 101
IRC 78
itlhomes 175
job pages 107
job sites 134
Jobdirect 137
Jobs Unlimited 136
johntynes.com 29
jungle.com 187
Ladbrokes 169
Land Registry 174
laptopshop.co.uk 182
lastminute.com 14, 184
latebreaks.com 185

lateral domain names 35
legal documents 106
legal issues 122
letsbuyit.com 31, 185
lewishamcentre.co.uk 181
link exchange 73
Links resouce sites 27
Lloyds TSB 130
long positions 156
Lotter-e 169
Magazine resource sites 29
making banners 71
market 42
marksandspencer.co.uk 181
masterfarm.co.uk 182
memberships 54
merchandise 109
moneyformail 112
mortgages 171
Motley Fool 163
movies 9
mp3 25
naming domains 117
NASDAQ 11
Nasdaq.com 26
Nationwide 131
Network Solutions 120
new domain extensions 126
next.co.uk 181
nominet 119
Onion magazine 15
online auctions 143
on-line discounters 176

INDEX

online gambling 164
online gaming 13
Open.gov.uk 17
order tracking 106
outlay 41
overheads 41
overseas banking 133
page size 51
peoplebank 135
personal promotion 138
personnel 41
planning 38
planning ahead 40
planning your site 20
porn sites 25
portals 10
postage agreements 150
principles.co.uk 181
product catalogue 105
professional web space 45
profit 41
profitability 96
programming 47
promoting your site 71
Promotional sites 22
property details on line 172
Public services 17
purchase circles 8
qxl 154
R&D Millennium 121
ragingbull 163
registered users 96
registering domains 34

registration 53
registration charges 121
relevant domain names 35
Resource sites 25
Response time 66
Reuters 11
reviews 8
Revland 29
reward scheme payments 114
reward schemes 110
rics 175
Sales sites 29
satire 15
schogini.com 45
schwab-worldwide 163
Scott Adams 12
SEC 102
second-hand goods 182
selftrade 163
selling a house 170
selling advertising 86
selling banner space 71, 82
selling email lists 81
selling shares 156
selling your site 98
sellmydomain.co.uk 123
services 105
share dealers on the net 159
share information 161
shares 155
shareware 16
shipping 186
shopping 176

short positions 156
showcasing 22
Sinclair Research 18
Site maps 64
Site-In-A-Box 50
solicitors 173
Spam sites 25
special offers 14
sponsoring lists 74
sponsorship 58, 82
spoof 15
sporting bets 168
stock floatation 101
stocks 155
strategy 38, 56
surfer reward schemes 110
surveys 173
swap shops 182
swapitshop.com 183
swapwell.com 183
Swiss-magic.ch 27
target market 42
technical complexity 53
tesco.com 181
tescodirect.com 178
text 51
TGP 25
themed resources 108
tied web space 44

Timely delivery 69
titleabsolute.com 175
tote online 169
trademarks 118
traditional media 76
tribute sites 21
turnover 96
UK specific domains 126
uksportscars.com 182
updates 61
URL 32
Usenet 75
user records 96
Utility resource sites 27
viewing lots 146
viral marketing 77
warez 25
waterstones.co.uk 181
web content 46
web programming 47
Web space 43
webswappers.com 183
Wharf.uk.net 121
William Hill offshore bookies 169
Wolf Network 50
world domains 126
writing 46, 51
yahoo auctions 153